BOROUGHBRIDGE IN WORLD WAR II

SECOND EDITION

Mike Tasker

© 2014, 2015 Mike Tasker. All rights reserved.
ISBN 978-0-9934703-0-1

First edition: December 2014.
Second edition: November 2015

Typeset in LaTeX by Datbatte Press.
Printed by CreateSpace.
Published by Datbatte Press, Chesham, England.

*To the people
of Boroughbridge and around,
then and now.*

Military Parade,

Boroughbridge, 1941

Contents

Preface ix

Acknowledgements xi

1 Introduction 1

2 Maps 5

I Active Service

3 Casualties 11

4 Active Servicemen Surviving The War 19

5 Doug Lofthouse's Photos from Malta 65

6 The Royal Canadian Air Force in Boroughbridge . . . 97

7 Women in the forces 101

8 Searchlight Batteries 107

9 Prisoners of War 109

10 Local Civilians Working For The Military 111

11 Women in war work 115

12 Bevin Boys 119

II The Services In Boroughbridge

13 Home Guard 123

14 Royal Observer Corps 127

15 Air Raid Precautions 129

16 Fire Service 131

17 Police and Special Constables 133

18 Civilian Ambulance Service 135

III Life In Boroughbridge

19 Evacuees 139

20 Domestic Life 143

21 Entertainment and Social Activities 149

22 The Bridge Collapse of 1945 153

23 Personal Memories 157

Index 175

Boroughbridge War Memorial

Preface

Preface to the second edition

I have been very pleasantly surprised by the reception the first edition of this book received following its publication just before Christmas in 2014. It was, as I noted then, more "published than finished", and yet it has received a wonderfully warm reception from residents of Boroughbridge past and present.

That has, in itself, brought new contacts and new stories, and I am pleased to be able to include a number of these in this revised edition. The book now includes over 270 biographical sketches, and reflects over 200 separate interviews along with follow-up.

My one real regret in the first edition was the lack of coverage of Minskip, very much a part of the Boroughbridge community. In this edition that has now been rectified: Minskip's treatment is now at proper par with those of Boroughbridge, Aldborough, Langthorpe, Kirby Hill and Roecliffe.

Other new material includes an aerial photo showing the town in early 1946, now used with permission from English Heritage; the carrier-pigeon service; and new material on the Royal Canadian Air Force whose presence was such a major factor in the town during the war. In addition there have been several corrections.

Still this can never be finished, and still we await more stories from the eventual opening of official archives.

—Mike Tasker

Knaresborough,
19th November 2015

Preface to the first edition

As a native of Boroughbridge born in New Row in 1936, I spent the earlier years of my childhood growing up in the Second World War period, quite close to the centre of town. My parents were Herbert and Dorothy Tasker, my older brother Colin and younger sisters Beryl and Joyce. The war was a background feature of my early childhood, I still have vivid memories of events in the town from that time.

The town had been such a hive of activity and so fully committed to the war effort. Lives were lost as its young men took part in actions all over the world, young women were conscripted into uniform or other war work, the air was buzzing with aircraft from local airfields, and soldiers were ever present with the army camps in the town. The civil defence organisations were constantly on the alert in case of a German invasion.

The prospect that the sacrifices and privations of those times could be forgotten has always been unthinkable to me.

Three things eventually prompted me to write about the war. Firstly I found a log book of the ARP from 1939-42 amongst the family papers left by my father when he died. I pondered what to do with it, as I thought it may have some historical value. Secondly when I recently joined the Boroughbridge Historical Society and browsed through the information they already had about the war, I was encouraged to find that many shared my desire to record the memories of that time, and that they had already made a good start, but realised that there was a lot more I could contribute. Finally I was spurred on further when I discovered that tourists who had relatives with wartime connections were coming to the town, some from remote parts of the UK, some from as far away as Canada, but I found that the Tourist Information Centre had no publications, and very little information to offer related to the war.

There were still people around the town who had direct knowledge of the wartime, although age was taking its toll, and memories were fading. I resolved to gather all the information I could, and to get it down on paper before memories disappeared for ever.

So, starting with names on the war memorials in Boroughbridge and the surrounding villages, and with friends, family and members of the Boroughbridge Historical Society, I began to interview people with knowledge and memories of the wartime. I have been able to interview over 120 people, mostly face-to-face, whose generously shared memories and stories, and especially their treasured photographs, have added colour and depth to those solemn lists of names which were my starting-point, and also the stories of many more men and women who took part in and survived the war. The result is over 200 biographical sketches of men and women from the Boroughbridge area who contributed to the war effort, together with a few longer accounts, and one fascinating story told in pictures.

I have felt that I owe it to those who have helped me, to make this volume available quickly. A book like this can never be complete, and after 18 months working on it I am painfully aware that I am publishing it, rather than finishing it.

Most of the stories told here are short. Perhaps that is fitting: many preferred to understate their war service, or to erase painful memories, while a few remained under obligations of secrecy. And, for any historian, more material also means more room for indiscretion or inaccuracy.

More stories could have been told. I have some contacts whom I have not been able to follow up yet. At the very beginning of the project it appeared to me that Minskip may already have been covered by suitable material and, regrettably, I have not included Minskip at all in this edition, though it is very much one of the villages in the Boroughbridge community along with Aldborough, Langthorpe, Roecliffe and Kirby Hill which are covered here.

Perhaps a future edition, or the opening of official archives (some time between 2020 and 2045, according to the ever-changing forecasts), may make good on some of these gaps.

Nonetheless I hope it is a fitting, if small and inadequate, tribute to those whose sacrifices brought us through those times, and that it will be of interest both to those with personal memories of the wartime, and to those growing up today in a very different world.

—*Mike Tasker*

Knaresborough,
17th November 2014

Acknowledgements

It has been a tremendous pleasure to work on this project, with old friends and contacts appearing as if from nowhere to help. I am grateful to all those I have spoken to who have given so generously of their time, providing the stories and photos which are the bulk of the material in the book. I have sought to acknowledge all these specifically throughout the text.

Thanks are also due to Cyril Wright, Geoff Craggs and Aidan Foster for their input and encouragement, particularly for their knowledge of local contacts, which were so helpful in the early stages of the work. Cyril, Geoff and Aidan also read the whole manuscript of the first edition in nearly its final form: I am grateful for the comments and corrections they made at this stage.

For the second edition I owe particular thanks to Mary March for her research and corrections, and to Eileen Lebert for information on the RCAF in the Boroughbridge area.

Doug Lofthouse's photos in Chapter 5 are a stunning visual record of the war as one Boroughbridge man encountered it. Along with their understated descriptions, they show something of the realities of the conflict. I am immensely grateful to Doug's son Mick Lofthouse for making this material available.

My thanks to Martin my son who has not only been most encouraging, but has also taken on the editing and publishing role for the book whilst still leading a very busy life at work and at home with his own family.

Despite all my care with sources and with proof-reading, and all the help I've had, I fear that some mistakes of understanding, or even of spelling, may yet have crept through. Of course these are my responsibility. I shall be happy to take any corrections, directly or via the Boroughbridge Historical Society.

While the work on this second edition has thankfully been at a more leisurely pace than that on the first edition, it has nonetheless taken time, and I am grateful as ever for the support and patience of those close to me, especially of my wife Christine.

Chapter 1

Introduction

Not since the Battle of Boroughbridge in 1322 has the town been the centre of such activity as it was in World War II. In those turbulent and exciting, but dangerous days, the town was a hive of activity. With its central location on the Great North Road, the town was an obvious location for an Army staging post, and in the late 1930s an Army camp was established in Boroughbridge Hall and its grounds. The Crown Hotel, Three Greyhounds, Three Horse Shoes, Windmill Cafe, Hotel Cottages, the Malt Shovel Inn and other locations were also occupied by the Army. Later there were Army Nissen huts between Springfield Road and York Road. There was constant activity and movement by soldiers, and with Dishforth Aerodrome just two miles away, Linton, Topcliffe and other airfields also close, aerial activity was ever present over the town throughout the war.

The town was on a war footing along with the rest of the country. Many young men and women from the Boroughbridge area served in all three of the armed services, in all theatres of the war. Some never returned. Others served in support services such as the Home Guard, ARP (Air Raid Precautions), ROC (Royal Observer Corps), Special Constables, fire fighters, ambulance drivers and others. A few local young men were even conscripted to work down the mines as "Bevin Boys". Lifeboats and Fire Control Boats were built at Boddy's Wood Yard. Evacuees were housed in the town during the bombing raids on our big cities.

Troop movements were continual. A number of regiments were billeted for short periods in the town over the length of the war period: local memories include the Royal Armoured Corps Tank Regiment, Devonshire Regiment, Pioneer Corps, Parachute Regiment, Kings Own Yorkshire Light Infantry (with their bugle badge), West Yorkshire Regiment, Liverpool and Scottish (with their kilts on parade), Shropshire Regiment, the Royal Army Medical Corps and others.

In the early days of the war, particularly in the 1941-42 period, there was regular enemy aerial activity in the area, keeping the ARP and local defence services very busy. There were several air crashes around the town, including a Lancaster in Aldborough which was a vivid early memory for me, and other Lancasters and Halifaxes. Later on mock battles were staged in the town, especially around D-Day, a source of great excitement for local young boys.

The local pubs were regularly frequented by the soldiers, and also airmen from Dishforth. The Black Bull seemed to be a particular favourite for the French Canadians, who left a huge maple leaf symbol on the roof of the fountain at the end of the war before they left for home. Dances were frequently held at the Crown Hotel, Hotel Cottages and the Parochial Hall, a regular attraction for the young soldiers, airmen and local girls. Numerous marriages resulted.

Young girls at the age of 19 were called up, some went into the forces, others worked at the armaments factories at Farnham and Thorpe Arch. For a rural community surprisingly few served in the Land Army.

The railway was kept busy as a hub for transporting troops and tanks to the local forces, and bombs for the local airfields.

Chapter 1. Introduction

Prisoners of war were a regular sight in the latter years of the war, many Italians and later on Germans. Some German PoWs were accommodated in the Old Brewery in Langthorpe, while both Italians and Germans were in the Springfield Army Camp. Italians and then German POWs were housed in the camp at Springfield Road when it was evacuated by the army.

Local young men in uniform took part in almost all theatres of the war. There were those who fought with the BEF (British Expeditionary Force) in the rearguard action in France and the evacuation from Dunkirk in 1940. One fought in the Battle of Britain—the "few", indeed. Many fought in the Desert war in North Africa against the Italians and later Rommel's Africa Corps. One survived the most intense and prolonged Axis bombing of Malta, in 1941-43. Then there was the invasion of Sicily and Italy. Local lads took part in bombing attacks on Germany and Italy with great distinction and tragic loss of life. D-Day and the follow-up invasion of Europe took many local soldiers and airmen into the conflict, and cost several local lads their lives.

Alongside the conflict in Europe and North Africa, there was the fight against the Japanese in the disease-ridden malaria-infested jungles of Burma. Several of our young men were involved there, in some of the most brutal fighting of the war.

At sea, there were some 20 local men in several roles around the world, including the action against the *Bismarck* and the sinking of the *Prince of Wales* battleship. Needless to say, there were also those who lost their lives at sea.

Some remained on the home front, for home defence, while others spanned the world from the Falkland Islands to Iceland, West Africa, Gibraltar, and India, Singapore and Burma in the East. Some made the ultimate sacrifice, several suffered serious wounds, others were taken prisoner of war.

Almost as a grand finale in Boroughbridge between VE and VJ day, the Great North Road bridge over the river Ure collapsed under the weight of a 180-ton load, on 5th July 1945, before the end of the war with Japan, causing serious dislocation to the Great North Road traffic. Boroughbridge was fortunate that the Army had previously built a Bailey bridge further downstream, which was used as an emergency river crossing, until a more substantial, but still temporary, bridge was erected upstream of the old bridge.

The hardships of the war were borne by the local residents, as with the rest of the country. Women often bore the brunt of day-to-day existence, coping with the shortages and rationing of many things, with many of their menfolk away on military service. There was however a close neighbourliness and community spirit quite unequalled in these later years.

This book tells that tale. For me the beginning was the war memorials in Boroughbridge, Aldborough, Kirby Hill and Langthorpe, Roecliffe, and later Minskip: in Chapter 3, 24 men who never returned are listed, as far as possible in the order they appear on the memorials, with what detail I could find of their service records and, wherever possible, a photograph. Then Chapter 4 gives similar information on about 180 men who did survive the war, having fought in all the armed forces, in all theatres of the war.

A remarkable find during my researches was Doug Lofthouse's photo album from his time on Malta—the most heavily bombed place in the world during the war. About 70 photos from his album, with Doug's understated comments, are given in Chapter 5.

Chapter 6 contains some stories and memories of the Canadians based in Dishforth (for the town's perspective on the Canadians, see some of the personal stories later in Chapter 23).

Chapter 1. Introduction

The remainder of Part I covers women in both military and civilian work, searchlight batteries, PoWs, local civilians working for the military, and Bevin Boys. These chapters highlight the degree to which World War II was "total war"; and where details are available, they are fascinating.

Boroughbridge itself was the host to many wartime services: Home Guard, Royal Observer Corps, Air Raid Precautions, along with wartime versions of fire, ambulance and police services. Part II gives a brief overview of those.

Part III becomes more personal. Chapters 19 and 23 give personal accounts of evacuees (from both sides of the story) and several people—children at the time—who grew up in Boroughbridge. There are several links between these chapters, not least Mary Smailes, the remarkable lady whose role was to place evacuees, and whose two daughters Elizabeth Thompson and Sheila Keighley have contributed their stories. Between these two chapters are snapshots of domestic life, the entertainments available at the time, and the collapse of the Great North Road bridge.

Chapter 1. Introduction

Chapter 2

Maps

General Situation

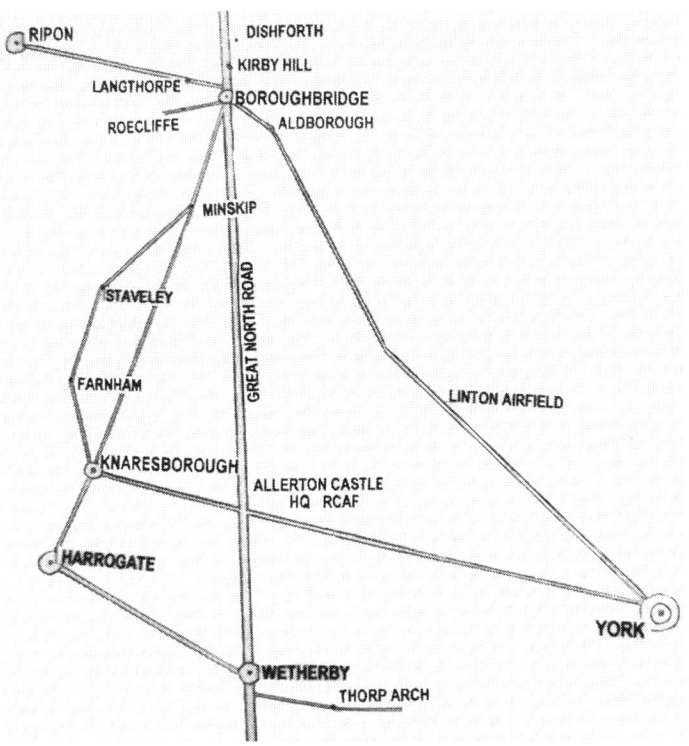

Boroughbridge is now comfortably bypassed by the A1M. For many years the Great North Road ran straight through Boroughbridge. This, together with the nearby airfield at Dishforth—still active today—was a significant factor in Boroughbridge's role in the Second World War.

The community around Boroughbridge is normally considered to include the historic Roman town of Aldborough (Isurium), Langthorpe, Roecliffe, Kirby Hill and Minskip.

During the war there were munitions factories at Farnham (just north of Knaresborough) and Thorp Arch (near Wetherby).

Central Boroughbridge   Chapter 2. Maps

Central Boroughbridge

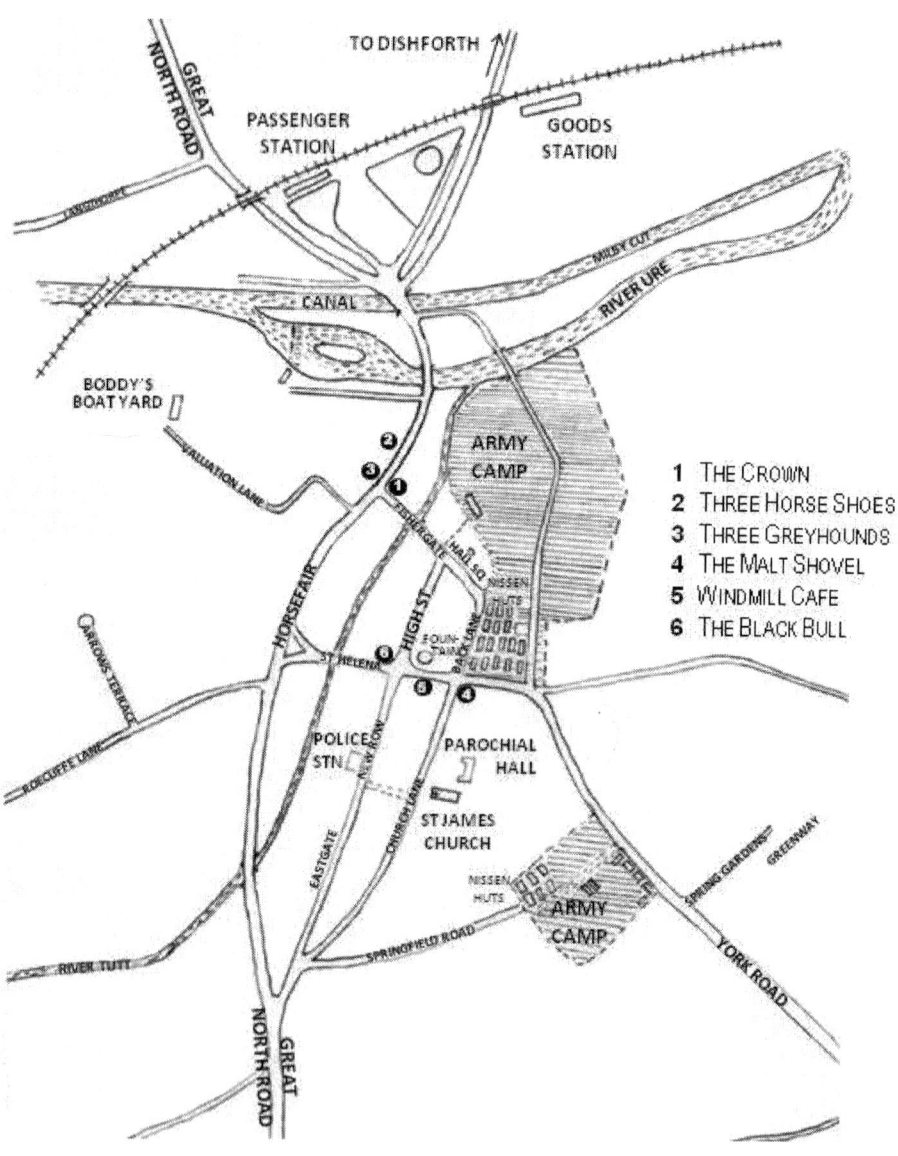

The central area of Boroughbridge was very small during the wartime, and augmented only slightly by the two army camp areas set up on the edge of town.

Chapter 2. Maps

Aerial Photo, 1946

Source: English Heritage (RAF Photography), used with permission
In this aerial photograph taken on 26th March 1946, the central area is seen. The remaining Nissen huts are hidden by trees. At the top, the collapsed Great North Road bridge and its temporary replacement can be seen.

Part I
Active Service

Chapter 3
Casualties

Boroughbridge

Ordinary Seaman Robert Broadbelt

Son of Robert and Ada Broadbelt, of Arrows Terrace, Boroughbridge. d 31/01/42 aged 30.
Royal Navy, service number P/JX 264211.
Served on HMS Belmont. The Belmont was a destroyer in the 3rd Escort Group which was torpedoed and sunk by the German submarine U-82 in the North Atlantic off Newfoundland. All 138 crew were killed.
Commemorated on Portsmouth Naval Memorial (Panel 65, column 2).

Sergeant Basil T Gault

Son of Allan Reid Gault and Doris Matilda Gault, of Springfield Road, Boroughbridge. d 20/09/44 aged 19.
Glider Pilot Regiment, Army Air Corps. Service number 2623833.

As the Allies advanced north towards the River Rhine, the British 1st Airborne Division, supported by The Glider Pilot Regiment and the Polish Independent 1st Parachute Brigade, landed at Arnhem to secure bridges over the Nederrijn. They met severe resistance, including the 9th SS and 10th SS Panzer Divisions. After four days the small British force which had reached the bridge at Arnhem was overwhelmed.
Commemorated on Arnhem Oosterbeek War Cemetery Memorial.

Flight Sergeant Dennis Myers

Son of Robert Christopher and Emily Myers of Eastgate, Boroughbridge. d 15/07/44, age 21.
Pilot. Service number 1217452.

290 Squadron, Royal Air Force Volunteer Reserve. In 1944 290 Squadron was based at Long Kesh in Northern Ireland. Its role was to facilitate the training of anti-aircraft gunners by towing drogues, and there were heavy demands for its services from the RAF Regiment, Army, Royal Navy and the USAAF gunnery school near Kilkeel, especially in the run-up to D-Day. It was transferred to Scotland in February 1945.

Buried Boroughbridge Cemetery, (Plot D, Grave 866A).

Sergeant George H Tilburn

Son of Stanley and Violet Tilburn, of 3 Arrows Terrace, Boroughbridge. d 06/10/44 aged 18yrs 6mths.
Air Gunner. Service number 1591010.
76 and 78 Squadrons, RAF Volunteer Reserve.
George had flown as mid-upper gunner on five bombing missions in September 1944 – Le Havre (Sept 10th), Gelsenkirchen (12th), Kiel (15th), Boulogne (17th), and Calais (26th).
His fatal 6th mission on 6th October took off at 1430 from RAF Breighton, near Selby, for a daylight bombing raid on Gelsenkirchen in Germany. En route to the target their aircraft collided in the air with another Squadron Halifax, both machines falling on, or near, the Dutch Reformed Church at Oude-Tonge (Zuid Holland) on the island of Overflakkee.

The crew of Sgt Tilburn's Halifax were: Flying Officer RL Stanley, Sgt GE Kemp, Sgt GW Habgood, Sgt JA McKillop, Sgt A Moss, Sgt H Lockett, Sgt GH Tilburn. Sgt Lockett is buried in Den Bommel General Cemetery.
Sgt Tilburn and the others lie in Bergen Op Zoom War Cemetery, Noord Brabant, Netherlands. (Reference 20, B2)
Source: George Bailes.

Gunner George (William Thomas) Hartley

Of Arrows Terrace, Boroughbridge. d 29/10/44, age 20.
Royal Artillery, service number 14333472, 186 Field Regt.
Killed by machine gun fire as he looked out from his armoured troop carrying vehicle during operation to clear the Scheldt estuary at the canal between North and South Beveland.

Buried at Kruiningen General Cemetery, Grave 158.
Source: Sister Olga (Hartley) Ekin

Chapter 3. Casualties

Boroughbridge

Fusilier Vivian G Kitching

Son of Benjamin and Harriet Kitching, of Spring Gardens, Boroughbridge. d 17/09/44, age 34.

1st Battalion, City of London Regiment, Royal Fusiliers. Service number 4624636.

Buried Florence War Cemetery, Tuscany, Italy.

Source: Nephew Dave Kitching

Captain Robert Ferguson Lees

Originally from Glasgow, but after joining the army, lived with his sister Mary Smailes in Boroughbridge when home on leave. d 1943.

RASC. Photo 7th May 1943.

He served in North Africa and died there of a liver infection.

Mary Smailes asked that he should be remembered on the Boroughbridge war memorial.

Source: Nieces Elizabeth (Smailes) Thompson and Sheila (Smailes) Keighley.

Richard "Sonny" Reed

Eastgate, Boroughbridge. d 1941.

Driver, attached to Royal Army Ordnance Corps.

Originally stationed at Dishforth, then transferred to London. Hit on the head by debris during a bombing raid in the blitz of 1940/41, got meningitis as a result, and died some 6 weeks later in London.

Source: Sister Julia Calley

Sapper Godfrey Craggs

Of Stump Cross, Boroughbridge. d 17/6/40, recorded on Aldborough War Memorial.
Royal Engineers.
He was one of thousands who died when the *Lancastria* was bombed and sunk off St Nazaire on 17th June 1940. The ship was overloaded with troops who had been cut off after the evacuation from Dunkirk.
Source: Son Geoffrey Craggs
(Geoffrey's wartime memories are told in Chapter 23, p157.)

Aldborough

Flight Ltn Andrew Thomas Lawson Tancred

Son of Lady M Lawson Tancred, Boroughbridge, d 14/1/44.

49 Squadron RAF Volunteer Reserve, S/N 101561.
Lancaster Bomber Pilot based at Fiskerton, near Lincoln. Shot down over Germany on bombing raid on Brunswick.
Remembered with honour, Hanover War Cemetery.

Leslie Pratt

d April 1945.
Army, Royal Fusiliers, served first in Egypt where he met his younger brother Geoffrey, transferred to Greece where he was badly injured by shrapnel, repatriated to England, hospital in St Albans, operated to remove shrapnel from main artery from heart to brain but did not survive the operation.
Buried May 1945 in Stillington Cemetery (precise dates not yet identified).
Source: Daughter-in-law Ruth Pratt and sister Mary Robinson.

Chapter 3. Casualties — Aldborough

Geoffrey Pratt

d 23/5/44, age 21.
4397302 Trooper, 51st Leeds Rifles, Royal Tank Regiment.

Served in Egypt, met his brother Leslie in North Africa, moved on to campaign in Italy, killed at Monte Cassino.
Buried in Monte Cassino Cemetery.

Source: Sister Mary Robinson

Corporal Richard Taylor

d 18/2/43.
Army, Royal Army Service Corps, S/N 4532046

Was part of BEF in France at outbreak of war in 1939, No 5 Sub Park, 2nd Ammunition Park BEF. Returned to England probably via evacuation from Dunkirk, and was immediately posted to Egypt.

Letters home from end October 1940 indicate he was in RASC Pack Transport. Was involved in several role changes whilst there, as the front line swung one way and then the other in the Western Desert war. Finally he was in 129 company RASC in Libya supporting the 32nd army Tank Brigade. His last letter home, dated 2nd June 1942, reported that he "just got here in time to be in the mix-up" and that it was thrilling and exciting. It must have been at Tobruk.

A later official letter indicated that he had gone missing on 20th June 1942, the date when Tobruk fell to the Germans and Italians, which must have been when he was taken prisoner.

He was taken to a PoW camp in Ancona, Italy. A letter from another soldier in the same camp indicated that the conditions there were terrible. The winter of 1942/3 was a very bad one in Italy. Richard died either from illness or starvation on 18th February 1943.

He is buried in Ancona military cemetery.
Source: Deduced from letters held by son Richard Taylor junior.

Warrant Officer Henry Halton Hawking

Son of Harold and Mary Kathleen Hawking, Ellenthorpe. d 3/8/45, age c30.
Service No 914339. Royal Artillery, 135 (The Hertfordshire Yeomanry) Field Regiment.
POW of the Japanese, Malaya; died in captivity. His family were notified of his death one day before the end of the war with Japan.
Recorded on Aldborough church war memorial.
Source: Elizabeth (Smailes) Thompson, confirmed Olive Duck, forceswarrecords.co.uk

Langthorpe

Sergeant Peter Harry Barrowclough (Barry) Green

Son of Douglas and Evelyne May Green, of Langthorpe, d 18/1/43.
RAF 76 Squadron, Sergeant Wireless Operator.
He was on a Halifax bomber flying from Linton-on-Ouse to bomb Berlin. The aircraft disappeared without trace.
The crew are commemorated on the Runnymede Memorial.

George Tubby

Son of Levi and Mary Tubby, husband of Molly Tubby, Langthorpe. d 17/9/40, aged 30.
Joined Navy as soon as he was old enough.
Leading Seaman, Service No C/JX127801.

His ship, HMS Kent, was a heavy cruiser, part of the Mediterranean Fleet which attacked the port of Bardia in Eastern Libya, 16th September 1940. It was attacked by Italian Savoia Marchetti SM79 torpedo bombers the next day, hit in the stern and badly damaged. George Tubby was almost certainly killed in this action. With great difficulty the Cruiser was towed back to Alexandria for repairs: it was out of action for a full year.
Recorded on Kirby Hill War Memorial
Source: Niece Mary Maybourne, and forceswarrecords.co.uk.

Petty Officer Harold Tubby

Son of Levi and Mary Tubby, Langthorpe. d 1944, age 33.
Royal Navy. D/JX 136042, Petty Officer.
Took part in the Dunkirk evacuation, his ship was the one which picked up Harold's brother Donald.
On the destroyer HMS Offa, participated in commando raid on Vaagso and Maaloy Islands off Norwegian coast, December 1941, and was mentioned in despatches.
Killed while serving on land base HMS Excellence 11, Durban, South Africa, in 1944, perhaps in an explosives accident.
Recorded on Kirby Hill War Memorial.
Source: Niece Mary Maybourne.

Kirby Hill

Sergeant Tom Calvert, DFM

d 2/1/44.
RAF, 101 Squadron, based Ludford Magna, Lincs. Rear gunner in bombers.
Killed in Lancaster SR-Z on bombing mission to Berlin.
His name is on the memorial in St James' Church along with Dennis Myers and George H Tilburn.
Source: Frank Whiting

Roecliffe

Pte Harry Cooper

Son of John William and Edith Cooper, Kirby Hill. d 26/9/1944, age 21.

Army, S/N 14278142. Gordon Highlanders 2nd Battalion.

Killed in Holland in September 1944. His parents were informed that their son was missing presumed dead.

Buried in Milo, Holland.

Source: Olive Duck, forceswarrecords.co.uk, Freda (Stott) Cooper.

William Baynes

Army, killed in action. No other information yet.

Eric Hannam

d 27/10/44, age 20.

7th Battalion Cameronians, Rifleman Service No 14329999.

Buried in Bergen op Zoom Cemetery.

Source: Margaret Turner, John and Rita Hannam

Sergeant Gilbert Crozier

d 30th September 1944, age 20.

Radio Operator/Air Gunner.

Had trained at Yatesbury. Died on a training flight, in a Stirling Bomber which took off from RAF Wratting Common near Cambridge, and crashed at Horse Heath, 12 miles south east of Cambridge, due to engine failure.

Source: Brother Johnny Crozier

Flight Lieutenant Michael Thomas Gibson Henry, DFC

Buried in Roecliffe Cemetery.

RAF, Service No 39876. d 13/1/1941, aged 28.

Son of T.G. Henry and Edith M. Henry of Compton Chamberlayne, Wiltshire. Husband of Elizabeth Marion Henry (Nee Ward). Was resident at the Crown Hotel, Roecliffe.

Bomber Pilot, flew with 35 Squadron, the first squadron to be equipped with the new Halifax Mk 1 bomber. Stationed at Linton-on-Ouse, his Halifax Mk 1 caught fire and crashed near Dishforth on a training flight. All crew were killed.

Lance Corporal William Edward Smart

Dorset Regiment, 2nd Btn, d 27/4/1944 in Burma, age 25.

Son of A P and Ethel Smart, husband of Barbara Adair Smart of Boroughbridge.

From the date of death it can be deduced that William Smart almost certainly lost his life in the battle for Kohima, one of the most savage battles of the whole war. Disease, heat exhaustion and food shortage were the background for this gruesome battle.

Recorded on Roecliffe Church War Memorial plaque.

Chapter 4
Active Servicemen Surviving The War

The men listed below saw active service in all the British armed forces, and in all theatres in which Britain fought.

Douglas "Doug" Lofthouse's remarkable photos from Malta, the most heavily bombed place in the entire war, are shown in Chapter 5, p65. Doug was awarded the Malta George Cross, as were all who endured that period.

The most highly decorated local man was Bernard Clayton (of Aldborough, p43), whose Distinguished Flying Cross, Conspicuous Gallantry Medal and Distinguished Service Order were earned in a war record which included a remarkable 82 bombing missions. After the war he flew 103 missions in the Berlin Airlift.

Quite apart from decoration, there are many fascinating records of local men's service. Even where I was unable to find no more than a name, the man concerned may have spent up to six years of his life away from home and been in frequent danger. The record in total is one of huge variety, commitment and sacrifice.

Boroughbridge

Douglas (Doug) Lofthouse

b09.11.1918, d23.05.2003.

In the RAF in Malta during WW2. Had a remarkable career as an Engine Fitter during the heavy bombing of 1941/3. He took amazing photos of the bombing of Valetta Harbour, airfields and other places. He survived the bombing himself although his accommodation block was bombed out. He survived the starvation period of mid 1942 when supplies to Malta could not get through. Awarded Maltese George Cross.

Note: Malta was the most bomb-damaged place in the world in 1941/2. See his photographs, Chapter 5.

Source: Mick Lofthouse, interview at WW2 Exhibition 11.05.13 and later.

Ken (Gus) Richardson

RAF mate of Doug Lofthouse.

Had Telephone Exchange at bottom of High Street. His sister was also in the forces.

Source: Cyril Wright, confirmed by Frank and Vera Whiting.

Charles Boddy

Engine Fitter in RAF 1942-45. Friend in RAF of Doug Lofthouse.

Source: Mick Lofthouse, confirmed Mary March

Eric Watson

Eastgate, Boroughbridge. b 1922.
RAF, Electrical Engineer, ground crew servicing bombers. Was in Singapore, then Ceylon during war.
Married WAAF Barbara Taylor. d1994.
Source: Jim Smith and Eric's son Mike Watson 21.07.2013, photo nephew Tony Watson

Cpl George Watson

Eastgate, b 1926. Eric Watson's younger brother.
RAF No 3041963. Enlisted 1944.
Initial training 1944 at Skegness, Oban, 3rd Squadron 255 ASR (Air Sea Rescue), then Kirkholm flying boat base near Stranraer.

Posted in 1944 to Barisal, India (now Bangladesh), flying boat base in the combat zone with the Japanese in Burma. Moved to Akyab, Burma, following the D-Day style landings there in January 1945. At the end of the war with Japan was posted to Koggala flying boat base in Ceylon.
It is probable that George was involved with the servicing of Sunderland Flying Boats.
Source: Son Tony Watson

Reginald Farrar

New Row, Boroughbridge.
Driver, RASC Army no. 194164.
In 8th army with Jack Clift in Western Desert. Photo, from the *Knaresborough Post* in 1942, shows Jack, Reg and two others (F Brown from Knaresborough and H Ibbotson from Grafton) in the desert, with their copy of the Knaresborough Post.

Fought at Tobruk, and unlike Jack who managed to get away in time, was captured in June 1942 and was PoW in Italy. Was working in the rice fields in Italy and escaped, but was recaptured and sent to POW camp in Austria. He escaped again, but was again recaptured, and spent the last days of the war in a German PoW camp, Stalag XI-B Fallingbostel, Lower Saxony, POW no 139957. The camp was liberated by the British Army on 16th April 1945, and the prisoners repatriated to England.

Chapter 4. Active Servicemen Surviving The War — Boroughbridge

This is the story related by Reg, now in the Riverside Court care home in Boroughbridge. He is now 99, (11th Feb 2014) profoundly deaf and difficult to communicate with, but very coherent, lucid and convincing when he realises what you want him to talk about. He has Charlie Lee, ex army, as a companion in Riverside Court, but neither Charlie nor Reg's wife knew that he was a POW in Italy also in Germany, nor that he had escaped twice.

His two brothers Vincent (Far East) and Bernard (Iceland), were both in the Army in WW2.

Sisters Bernice, ATS and Vivian, nurse.

Source: Reg (as above), also his wife Muriel Farrar (93); photo cutting from Knaresborough Post 1942; Sandra Clift.

Vincent Farrar

New Row, Boroughbridge.
Army, Far East.
Source: Muriel Farrar

Bernard Farrar

New Row, Boroughbridge.
Army, Iceland.
Source: Muriel Farrar

Percy Clift

Royal Engineers.
Friend of Doug Lofthouse in forces.

Percy was in Cairo July 1942, Beirut and (?) India in 1943 or 1944, and probably in Lagos, Nigeria in July 1944. (Deduced from photos with descriptions written not by him, probably his mother.)

Source: Sandra Clift

Lance Corporal Jack Harrison Clift

Service No T179525. Driver, RASC.

Initial training in Mansfield 1940, also Evesham later 1940

Served in 8th Army in the Western Desert, North Africa from 1941, photos from Alexandria, Mersa Matruh, and Cairo (Egypt), June 1941 - March 1942, Tobruk (Libya) June 1942, Burg el Arab August 1942, Tripoli 1942/43, Derna 1943. Then in Italy: Vasto Marina Sept 1944, Rome Oct 1944, Jesi March 1945, Naples March 1945, Forli May 1945, Venice May 1945.

Source: Sandra Clift

Pte Norman Spenton Robinson

3 Eastgate, Boroughbridge.
Army.

Source: Article in Newspaper (Knaresborough Post?) Recording death of Geoffrey Pratt. Also confirmed by Mary March.

21

Captain Jack Sharples

Army, Airborne Division.
Was in Boroughbridge, billeted with Pinkney's, Mill Lane. Associated with Boroughbridge Hall army camp prior to D-Day. Participated in D-Day landings, lost his arm through shell fire in France, trying to rescue a colleague.
After the war, had a men's outfitters shop in High Street.
Source: Gillian Sharples, Joyce Coates

Leslie Mudd

Eastgate. b 1923.
Army no 4538264. He enlisted Sept 1939, 1/5 Battalion West Yorkshire Regiment (despite being only 16 years old, if his birthdate above is correct). Transferred 19/1/1940 to Para 383(V)(a) Kings Reg.

Served in India, and was almost certainly involved with battles against the Japanese at Kohima and/or Imphal. His sister Dorothy remembers him saying "It was awful, there were dead bodies everywhere, and he (Leslie) drove a bulldozer to move dead Jap bodies into a pit".
Source: Sister Dorothy (Mudd) Coleman

Jimmy Capstick

New Row, Boroughbridge.
Enlisted in West Yorks Regiment in York for initial training, then transferred to the 1st Northamptonshire Yeomanry attached to RAC tank regiment. Truck driver supplying tanks with petrol and shells following Normandy Landings and their follow-up to Caen. Followed right through to Germany to the end of the war.
Demobbed quickly at the end of the war. As a time served joiner, involved with the refurbishment of neglected installations at Dishforth.
Source: Michael Wilson

Fred Wilson

New Row, Boroughbridge.

Chapter 4. Active Servicemen Surviving The War — Boroughbridge

REME. Enlisted early in war and was with the BEF in France, evacuated from Dunkirk.

At Normandy landings was driving an armoured bulldozer clearing the beaches along with Canadian Army. Followed the front with the army to Caen where he was involved in clearing a way through after the fall of Caen.

Subsequently involved in preparing auxiliary airstrips as the front moved onwards towards Germany. Sustained shrapnel wound to shoulder as his bulldozer was shot up by a German plane, but was not seriously injured and continued in action through to Germany and the end of the war.

Source: Michael Wilson, Fred's son.

Flew Mosquitos in aerial photography reconnaisance and pathfinder roles. Based on the Isle of Wight. Participated in attacks on V1 flying bombs by tipping wings to divert them away from their target. Survived being shot up more than once. Finished service at Marston Moor.

Source: Mary March, Roger Pybus

Sergeant Roland Patrick (Paddy) Atkinson

Eastgate, Boroughbridge.

Served in the Royal Observer Corps at outbreak of the war, then called up 1941.

RAF ground crew radar, Cranwell, Orkneys, then Krefeld, Germany. Met Henry Kissinger, then US Secretary of State for Defense, while in the RAF in Germany after the war.

Source: Peter Binns, daughter Rose (Atkinson) Walkinshaw

Jimmy Lawn

Squadron Leader Claude William Smith Pybus

Volunteered for RAF. Initially a rear gunner, graduated to Pilot.

New Row, Boroughbridge. Army, Driver in West Yorkshire Regiment.

23

Was in Falkland Islands 1941-43, then South Africa, then Burma to the end of the war.

After the war, Jimmy told Ian Hick that in Burma, he had had to drive a lorry carrying provisions to a unit on front line, but when he arrived at the destination it was deserted, nobody to be seen anywhere. He therefore decided to drive back to base. When he got back he was told that the Japanese had overrun the unit he was driving the supplies to, the front line had moved. Unwittingly Jimmy had driven right through the front line and back again without knowing and without seeing a soul. He had been lucky indeed.

Source: Ian & Wendy (Lawn) Hick

Cliff Calley

RAOC. Originally from Liverpool, attached to Tank Regiment of the Royal Armoured Corps in Boroughbridge, on provisions supply and servicing equipment.

As a trained upholsterer, involved in mending tents, covers and repairing other equipment.

Julia Reid met him in November 1940, they were quickly married in April 1941, just before he was posted abroad. (Middle East) She was just 19 years old. Cliff was abroad for the rest of the war.

Source: Julie Calley (91) Penny (Grayson) Harrison, Alan Calley (Cliff's son.) & Kate

Captain Jack Keighley

St Helena.

Royal Artillery.

Served in Burma. At the war's end was involved in guarding Japanese POWs. Japanese officers were billeted in Changhi Jail, Singapore, where the Japanese had previously held British POWs.

When he returned from Burma he had lost a lot of weight, was emaciated, his skin was yellow through the use of Quinine for treating malaria.

Source: Sheila (Smailes) Keighley

Wing Commander Herbert Walton

In RAF pre-war. Pilot in Fighter Command throughout war.

Wife Mary Walton. After the war, worked briefly in family grocers shop on High Street, then drove bus for Dodsworths.

Source: Geoff Craggs

Chapter 4. Active Servicemen Surviving The War — Boroughbridge

Thomas (Tony) Steele

Eastgate.
Army, Pte, 1st Btn Green Howards from 15th Dec 1939 - 28th March 1946.
Served in France, Italy, and Germany, involved in transporting men to the front line.
Sustained a shrapnel wound to his leg in Italy, and while recovering there witnessed the eruption of Mount Vesuvius. The piece of shrapnel, 1" long, was removed from his hip when he was 60. It was kept by his wife as a souvenir.
After the war he was a driver for the famous WW2 singer Vera Lynn when she went to Europe to entertain the troops.

Source: Mick Clift, also his son Anthony Steel. Also Tony's wife Doreen (née Wood), & daughter Yvonne Lawn.

Sgt Fred Steele

Eastgate, Boroughbridge.
Army.
Involved in mopping up operations, dealing with snipers etc as front line moved forward in Europe.

Source: Sister-in-law Doreen Steele, and Tony Watson

Fred Mudd

New Row.
Pte F. Mudd 13096649 187 SECC10CMF 150
In army throughout the war, in the Mediterranean area, probably North Africa.

Source: Pat (Leeming) Rowntree (niece).

Sgt Tom Lofthouse

New Row.
Army, RASC.

Served in Egypt from 1941. Probably followed up with the invasion of Italy until demob in 1945.

Source: Daughter Maria Lofthouse

Sgt Alf Stokes

Arrows Terrace.

b1920 in Wales, was in the Territorial Army before the war, then in the Devonshire Regiment. Was in Gibraltar early in the war, returned to England, stationed in Boroughbridge, met and married 18 year old Mary Smith (Jim's Sister) in 1943, then posted to India (see photo), then on to Burma where he spent the rest of the war.

Source: Pat Smith

Reg Tucker

Army, Devonshire Regiment, friend of Alf Stokes.

Served in Italy, part of the time with Gurkhas probably took part in the amphibious landings at Porto San Venere. The 2nd Devonshire Regiment was returned to England, amalgamated with the 50th Northumberland Infantry Division, trained for the invasion of Europe and participated in the D-Day landings at Gold Beach on 6th June 1944, suffering heavy casualties.

Married Margaret Mortimer from Spring Gardens. They lived in Arrows Crescent. Reg was treasurer of British Legion, Boroughbridge, after the war.

Source: Mick Lofthouse, also Elizabeth Knott

Chapter 4. Active Servicemen Surviving The War

Billy Weaver

Army Regular, Shropshire Regiment at Boroughbridge Hall.
Did service in Jamaica.
Met and married Nellie Binns,
Source: Cyril Wright, Janet Weaver

John (Jock) Richmond

Born Dumbarton 1920.
Army, Commandos.
In the evacuation from Dunkirk, was in the sea for a long time waiting in the queues for rescue boats.
Trained at Speen Bridge Commando training unit in Scotland. Fought with Lord Lovat, 4th Commandos, possibly in the Dieppe raid and also at the Sword Beach D-Day landings. Suffered shrapnel wounds but not seriously injured.
Eventually posted to Boroughbridge, where he met and married Joan Drury, 9th August 1945.

Jock was not one to talk much about his war-time experiences.
Source: Elizabeth (Smailes) Thompson, daughter Janet Young, Cyril Wright.

Reg Large

Royal Navy engine mechanic. Was on the North Atlantic and Russian convoys.
Reg had a real story to tell, interviewed him recently but he was very difficult to follow. Married Barbara Gault.
Source: Interview 06.06.2013, then later info from his son Stephen.

Sgt Don Murdoch

St James' Square.
Army, Royal Artillery. Served in North Africa and Italy.
Married Violet Taylor.
Source: Daughter Christine (Murdoch) Sillman

Richard Smith

Despatch rider in Service Corps in North Africa. Took messages from 1st Army to 8th army (Montgomery's) as they joined forces in Desert War. Later served in Italy and eventually into Germany.
Source: Brother Jim Smith, WW2 Exhibition 11.05.2013

Wilfred L "Whippet" Binns

Eastgate, Boroughbridge, Army Catering Corps.

Was stationed on off shore forts in Thames Estuary and also in Sittingbourne, Kent, in support of defence against bomber, buzz bomb attacks and also naval attacks against London.

Opened fish & chip shop on Horsefair after the war.
Source: Son Peter Binns

Henry Wombwell

RAF, Barrage balloon deployment from beginning of war. Based at Boston Spa, but deployed in London Docks and Hull fish docks during the heavy bombing. He happened to be in Coventry on a visit during the heavy bombing when the Cathedral was destroyed.

The very popular Fish & Chip shop in Boroughbridge High St during war was run by his father Percy.
Source: Peter Binns, Andrew Wombwell

William Watson

Horsefair.
Army, RASC, enlisted 1942.

Was not A1 medically because of flat feet. Was driver for a Lieutenant Colonel in Wiltshire but spent time at Malvern in Air Despatch, loading supplies and munitions onto aircraft for delivery to fighting forces on the continent.
Source: Son Dave Watson

Harold Pearson

Kirby Hill. Hugh's brother.

Joined the Royal Navy 1936. Leading Sick Berth Attendant on the Prince of Wales, the most modern battleship in the Royal Navy.

Had an eventful year in 1941. Took part in engagement with the German Battleship Bismarck in May 1941, when the ship was damaged by shell fire from Bismarck and Prinz Eugen, although the Bismarck was in turn hit by Prince of Wales shell fire. The Royal Navy flag ship HMS Hood was sunk in this action.

In August the Prince of Wales sailed with Winston Churchill to Newfoundland for a meeting with President Roosevelt, resulting in the Atlantic Charter agreement.

In September the ship escorted a supply convoy from Gibraltar to Malta, without incident.

The ship then set off for the far East, stopping over briefly at Capetown, South Africa for a refit in November. It then sailed for Singapore, but on 10th December was attacked and sunk, along with HMS Repulse, by Japanese torpedo bombers off Malaya. Harold was a survivor, picked up by a Royal Navy destroyer, possibly HMS Endeavour, luckily avoiding capture by the Japanese.

Spent the next 2 years in Johannesburg, South Africa.

Source: Ann (Pearson) Nelson, also Olive Duck, daughter Mrs Mary Knox.

Hugh Pearson

Church Lane, Boroughbridge.

In RAF, ground crew. In total served 22 years in the RAF, including several years in Germany after the war.

Source: Ann (Pearson) Nelson, Peter Nelson

Jack Varley

Woodwork teacher Boroughbridge Senior School.

Army, Royal Signals, in Egypt, alongside John Benson from Roecliffe. Ironically John had been taught by Jack, but John was now a sergeant, Jack a private soldier, so Jack was now the junior. John had to overcome his automatic inclination to call him "Sir".

Source: Cyril Wright, Geoff Craggs

Maurice Calvert

Sports and maths teacher, Boroughbridge Senior School.
Army in Egypt.
Source: Cyril Wright

Stan Morten

Fishergate.

Army, India—Royal Signals
Source: David Barley

Eric Frape

Son of Harold (Gaffa) Frape, Head Master, Boroughbridge Junior School.

Royal Navy, joined up 31st July 1944

Eric served on aircraft carrier HMS Pursuer, Feb 1945 - Jan 1946.

Source: Daughter-in-law Julie Frape, married to son Colin.

Cpl Robert Edward (Bob) Richardson

Spring Gardens, b 1909.
Army no. 14682540.
Prior to call-up, served in Auxiliary Fire Service. Enlisted November 1943, did training in Dorset with Tank Regiment, then served with Royal Armoured Corps in Middle East. In Egypt and Libya as part of the occupation forces, firstly as a regimental policeman, then took over responsibility for regimental fire service and equipment.
Demobbed 9/1946. After the war worked on road building and was killed in a hit-and-run incident on the Great North Road in the 1950s.
Source: Daughter Joan (Richardson) Neesam

RSM Arthur Richardson

Station View, Langthorpe. Bob's younger brother.

An army regular, enlisted early in the war, served in India and Burma.
Source: Niece Joan (Richardson) Neesam

Jack Lumsden

Spring Gardens, Boroughbridge.
Army, Pioneer Corps.
Known to have served in Gibraltar, probably other countries too. Came back to UK on the Mauritania, demobbed Dec 1946.
Source: Kathleen (Lumsden) Busby, Olga (Hartley) Ekin

Ernest Busby

Army, served with Chindits in Burma. Went missing presumed dead in the Burmese jungle, and turned up six months later.
Worked in Atkinson's coal yard after the war.
Source: Sue Kitching, Kathleen (Lumsden) Busby

Tom Leeming

Army, Service no.1695680, Royal Artillery.
Known to have served in North Africa. Sent presents home from Tripoli during the war.
Source: Wife Nancy (92), Pat (Leeming) Rowntree

Warrant Officer Maurice Holtby

Stump Cross, Boroughbridge.
Joined RAF March 1939, aged 22. Trained as flight mechanic at Dishforth and St Athan. (Author's note: he must have been selected for training on the Pratt & Whitney engines used in the American/Canadian Catalina flying boat, used by the RAF for antisubmarine patrols).

Further training in Canada December 1940 to June 1942. Back to St Athan for training as a flight engineer and air gunner. Promoted to Sergeant, posted to operational unit at Alness seaplane base near Invergordon. There he met Muriel Scaife, also from Boroughbridge, whom he married in June 1944. Flew antisubmarine patrols in Catalina flying boats over the Atlantic.

Transferred to Gibraltar Sept 1943, again in Catalina antisubmarine patrols. Shot down by German fighter over Bay of Biscay, took to a life raft along with other survivors and within 24 hours was picked up by Royal Navy and returned to Gibraltar.

Must have spent some time in Italy as his campaign medals include the Italian Star.

Returned to UK in June 1944, transferred to Killadeas seaplane base in County Fermanagh where he served as a flight engineer instructor, and in March 1945 was promoted to Warrant Officer. Subsequently transferred to a Liberator bomber squadron (they had the same Pratt & Whitney engines as the Catalina) in the Bengal region of India as part of South East Asia Command. There he spent the last few weeks of the war taking part in the Burma campaign.

Finally returned to Boroughbridge in Nov 1945. After the war, he served another 3 year period in the RAF as flight engineer on Sunderland flying boats at Pembroke Dock and Kai Tak in Hong Kong.

Tragically, in May 1955 he was killed in a road traffic accident near Kelly's Café on the old A1 in Boroughbridge.

Source: Son Dr Ian Holtby

Leonard Robinson

Stump Cross.
Army, Royal Engineers. Unlike Godfrey Craggs, escaped from St Nazaire in 1940, turned back from Lancastria because it was full. He was lucky indeed: he came back on another ship. Spent most of the war in movement control in Oxford. He had been on the railways in civilian life: was this what he was doing in Army?

Tragically knocked off his bike and killed shortly after the war, again on the old A1.

Source: Susan Robinson

Norman Ward

Stump Cross, Boroughbridge.
2205292 AC1 Ward. RAF Ground Crew, Aircraft Electrician. After initial training in Blackpool, Doncaster, Kerton Lindsay, sailed from Liverpool in January 1944 to West Africa.

Stationed at Jui camp, Sierra Leone, servicing Sunderland flying boats in Coastal Command. Also in Lagos Nigeria and Ivory Coast.

After war served in Malta, where he had to service Lord Louis Mountbatten's plane, and also to do guard whilst he slept. Visited Rome in transit.

Source: Wife Nora (Mallerby) Ward

Sgt Geoffrey Clayton

Hall Square.
RAF.
Probably Air Gunner. Enlisted in RAF same time as Norman Ward who took this photo of him.
Source: Norah Ward, Jim Smith

Gordon Clayton

Hall Square. Geoffrey's brother.
Royal Navy.
Married Dorothy Burley.
Source: Mary March

Sgt Donald Akers

Sergeant in the Royal Air Force Medical Service.
Spent most of the War in Ghana, Africa. Probably stationed at RAF Takoradi. He was involved in the treatment and research into treatment of the many diseases which people caught during the North African and Burma campaigns, such as malaria, yellow fever and others. Not involved in any military action throughout the war.
Source: Sue (Akers) Tiffany

Cpl Kenneth Akers

Minskip Road, Boroughbridge. b24.Sept 1919.
Marine Commandos. Enlisted Feb 1940 at Exeter. Clerk recording operational commands, Portsmouth. Demobbed 4th Jan 1946.
Married Isobel Alder Tibbie, Kelso, 17.01.1942.
Source: Daughter Sue (Akers) Tiffany

Dennis Slater

Royal Navy. Officer, rose to quite a senior level, probably in a technical capacity.
Brian (Busty) Slater's brother.
Source: Cyril Wright / Gwennyth (Robson) Bird

Boroughbridge

Jimmy Thomas

Corporal in RAF, ground crew at Dishforth.

Married Margaret Herron, Cora's sister. Their son is a barber in Boroughbridge.

Source: Cora (Herron) Hammond

William "Wally" Hammond

RAF ground crew, air frame fitter, stationed at Dishforth.

Chapter 4. Active Servicemen Surviving The War

Married Cora Herron.

Source: Cora (Herron) Hammond

George Hughes

Army, West Yorkshire Regiment. Army No 4540151.

Was from Dishforth, involved in the construction work at Dishforth aerodrome prior to enlistment. Enlisted early in the war, sent to France with BEF.

Married Cora Herron's sister Edna in 1940 on a special 3 day licence before his posting to France. Edna had to work at Farnham factory to keep the household going.

Escaped from Dunkirk by swimming out to a small boat, despite the fact that he was known not to be a swimmer before the war. Was picked up from the sea entirely naked but unharmed, dragged on to a small boat and returned to England.

Posted to Egypt, captured by the Italians in the Western Desert in late 1940, spent $4\frac{1}{2}$ years as POW, first in Italy then later in Germany in Stalag 344 Lamsdorf, Silesia, POW no. 28959.

Chapter 4. Active Servicemen Surviving The War — Boroughbridge

In January 1945 was on the three-month long forced march west without food to avoid the Russian advance. Conditions were appalling as described in Lawrence Bowes entry (p47). Was starving when liberated with the Allied advance, had to be fed gradually to re-adjust to food when he came home.

Lived with his wife Edna in Arrows Terrace after the war.
Source: Cora (Herron) Hammond.

Charles Herbert Herron

Army, Royal Armoured Corps.
Injured in Western Desert, had his heel blown off, sent to South Africa for treatment and recuperation.
Source: Sister Cora (Herron) Hammond

Sid Herron

In RAF abroad, Egypt.
Source: Sister Cora (Herron) Hammond

Fred Herron

1st Airborne Division, Fred hated being in the army. Developed a hernia and was hospitalised prior to operation Market Garden and the catastrophic para drop on Arnhem. Would not talk about the war.

Married Florence Shafer, sister to Mary (Shafer) Pearson, Hughie Pearson's wife.
Source: Ann (Pearson) Nelson & Cora Hammond, John Herron, Janet (Herron) Robinson, Kitty (Herron) Mole.

Gunner Bob Horner

Photo shows Bob receiving his World War II medals from General Collin in 1975.
Roecliffe Lane, Boroughbridge
Royal Artillery, Army no 1136919
Bob was involved in some of the most horrendous fighting of the war, against the Japanese in Burma.

35

Before call-up was helping to build Thorpe Arch munitions factory. Conscripted end 1941, initial training Pennypot camp Harrogate, then posted to Bombay (took 8 weeks to get there by ship via South Africa, as the troop ship zigzagged in the Atlantic to avoid U-boats).

After short training and acclimatisation in India, was posted to Burma. Fought with Wingate's Chindits in brutal fighting against the Japanese in malaria infested jungle of the Battle of the Admin Box (February 1944). The fighting was in jungle enclaves where they were surrounded by Japanese, their only supplies being delivered by air drops from the RAF and American Air Force. This was followed by the horrific Kohima/Imphal battles of March-July 1944.

Eventually in 1945 took part in the liberation of the Rangoon PoW camp. After rounding up Japanese prisoners in Bangkok at the end of hostilities, was homeward bound from Singapore when his boat hit a mine in shark infested waters. Fortunately the boat did not sink and he was able to continue his journey home, arriving back in the UK for demob in 1946.

During his service in Burma he had malaria four times and dysentery numerous times.

Bob briefly met up with his brother Cliff whilst he was in Burma, also his friend Con Lowther.

Source: Son Chris Horner, brother Ray Horner.

Pte Cliff Horner

Was in Territorial Army before the war, enlisted with the Cameron Highlanders at outbreak of war, posted to Burma, spent 4 1/2 years there.

Source: Ray Horner.

RSM (Quartermaster) Sergeant Ron Horner

Was in RASC Regiment, in supply group following D-Day landings, with Army through France, into Germany, finished up in Berlin.

Married a German girl 8 years later, stayed there for the rest of his life.

Source: Ray Horner.

Herbert (Bert) Clayton

Arrows Terrace.

Army, Durham Light Infantry.

Wounded in France three times after D-Day landings, spent long period in hospital in France and returned to Boroughbridge on crutches. He had shrapnel splinters in his body for the rest of his life.

He was from a family of 13 children. Bert's brothers Bill, Albert & Tom also in army (see below), sister Belle in ATS, elder sister Mary worked in Farnham Munitions Factory.

Source: Cyril Wright, Kath (Clayton) Proctor, Ann (Clayton) Orr

Chapter 4. Active Servicemen Surviving The War — Boroughbridge

Bill Clayton

Arrows Terrace.
Army. West Yorkshire Regiment. Served in Iceland.
Source: Sister Ann (Clayton) Orr, niece Maureen Deignan

Cpl Albert Clayton

Arrows Terrace.
Army, RASC.
Drove a gun carriage, and was also a dispatch rider in Germany.
Source: Sister Ann (Clayton) Orr, niece Maureen Deignan

Tom Clayton

Arrows Terrace.
Army, Royal Artillery.
Served in Italy.
Source: Sister Ann (Clayton) Orr, niece Maureen Deignan

Sgt Jack Burks

Arrows Terrace.
Army, West Yorkshire Regiment.
Was in TA before the war, called up at outbreak of war into West Yorkshire Regiment.
Posted to Iceland, and while there was involved in an accident, hit by a lorry on the job, as a result of which he was rendered deaf. Sent back to UK and invalided out.
After some time his hearing improved, but was refused for re-enlistment in the army in case his deafness returned. Spent the rest of the war working in John Brown's shipyard in Glasgow.
Source: Son Ross Burks, Gwenneth (Robson) Bird

Morris Robson

Arrows Terrace.
Sapper, Royal Engineers.
After training in England was sent straight to Sicily, took part in invasion, then on to Monte Cassino. Respite in Africa, then sent to France for D-Day and follow up.

Bernard (Bunny) Campbell

Lived near Blinking Owl, Boroughbridge. Vet's son.
Rear gunner in RAF.
Source: Cyril Wright

Sgt Frank A Wilson

Army No 5620389.
Army, Devonshire Regiment at Boroughbridge Hall. Friend of Alf Stokes.
Physical Training instructor. Known to be in Gibraltar 1943, probably also in Burma.
Married Winnie Steel.
Source: Nephew Anthony Steel.

Bob Spearman

Arrows Terrace.
Army. Trumpet player.
Source: Peter Binns

Sgt Bernard Harcourt

Army. Stationed in Boroughbridge, bandsman.
Married Joan Davy from Chocolate Buffet.
Source: Geoff Craggs

John Wynn

Army.
Married Vera Kitchen.
Source: Ruth Wardell

Sgt Jack Robshaw

Arrows Terrace/Eastgate, Boroughbridge.
Army, RASC. Fought in Desert War, North Africa, possibly Italy and finished up in Germany. Became a driving instructor. Served 12 years in the regular Army.
Source: Colin Tasker, Dave Kitching, Olga Ekin, sister Joyce (Robshaw) Parkinson.

Chapter 4. Active Servicemen Surviving The War   Boroughbridge

Owen Kitching

Eastgate, Boroughbridge, b1906.
Army, West Yorks Regiment. Served in France and Germany.
Source: Son Dave Kitching

Harold Kitching

Eastgate, Boroughbridge, b1901.
Army.
Source: Nephew Dave Kitching

Frank Lonsdale

Army.
Friend of Con Lowther.
Source: Janet (Lowther) Bennett

Roy Taylor

St James's Square.
RAF. Ground Crew, served in the UK.
Source: Neice Ann (Taylor) Fisher, Mary March

Jack Taylor

St James's Square.
RAF. As a builder by trade, involved in building maintenance, runway repair etc. Service in the UK, also in Hamburg at the end of the war, was witness to the complete devastation to the city.
Source: Daughter Ann (Taylor) Fisher, Mary March

Billy Smith

High Street.
Army.
Source: Mary March

Les Smith

High Street.
RAF, enlisted towards end of war.

39

Source: Cyril Wright

Tommy Blakeborough

Eastgate
Army.
Source: Mary March

George Sawford

Richmond, Surrey.
Cook, probably Army Catering Corps.
Stationed at Boroughbridge Army Camp, probably throughout the war.
Source: Daughter, at Aldborough and Boroughbridge Show, 20/7/14

Phil Taylor

From Liverpool.
Pipe Major in Liverpool Scottish regiment stationed in Boroughbridge.
Married Mollie Kershaw in St James' Church.

Source: Cyril Wright

Pte George J Berry

184th Field Ambulance 138th Brigade, 46th Division 1st Army.   Army No 7365842.
Joined the Army's RAMC in 1939, did basic training at Boroughbridge, billeted in the Malt Shovel. Attached to 8th Armoured Division with light Valentine tanks. Served in Algeria with 1st Army attacking Rommel's Desert Army from the west. After reaching Tunisia, followed through to the Italian Campaign landing at Salerno, through Naples, to Monte Cassino where he witnessed the bombing of the Abbey. After brief rest in Cairo back to Italy to the end of the war.

Ernest Sampson

Born in Leeds, Joined Territorial Army in April 1939, Called up in September at age 19 into 147th Field Ambulance unit, initial training at Boroughbridge but billeted at Ornhams Hall.
Involved with transport for Field Ambulance.

Cpl Raymond Porter

RAF.
Chef in the RAF. Spent 3 years in Burma, probably in the thick of the jungle fighting and probably often behind the enemy lines.
After the war, ran the Three Horse Shoes with his brother Eddie.
Source: Son Bernard Porter

Sgt Eddie Porter

RAF.
Instrument fitter with expertise in compass adjustment and maintenance. Spent the war in home postings.
After the war, ran the Three Horse Shoes with his brother Ray.
Source: Nephew Bernard Porter

Cpl James Henderson

RAF. Service no 1044279.
Fishergate, Boroughbridge.
RAF ground crew, signals. Served at Bridlington, Cranwell and Wittering. Briefly in the RAF Regiment, up to and following the Normandy landings, then transferred back to RAF Signals. Served in France, Belgium, Holland and Germany to the end of the war.
Jim was Clerk to the Council in Boroughbridge several years after the war.
Source: Margaret (Henderson) Urwin

Arthur Lindsey

Stump Cross, Army.
Was sergeant in Territorial Army before the war, joined West Yorks Reg but transferred to Royal Artillery.
Served on south coast throughout the war (probably on anti-aircraft), suffered ear damage as a result of gunfire.
Source: Mary (Lindsey) Wood

John Lindsey

Roecliffe Lane.
Was in the Territorials before the war, enlisted in the West Yorkshire Regiment at Strensall, York at the outbreak of war. Was batman for officers, spent the war in the UK, partly in the Nottingham area.
Source: Mary (Lindsey) Wood

Johnny Brown

Born in Telford.
Enlisted in Shropshire Light Infantry. Training at Ornham's Hall, south of Boroughbridge. Met and married Dorothy Watts, Tommy Watts's sister at Minskip Church, 1943.
Took part in the Normandy landings in the first wave of the invasion force on D-Day. Suffered a slight neck wound in the subsequent fighting.
Source: Vaughan Watts

Harry Ramsdale

Army.
Had a rough war, did not talk about it. Ran butcher's shop in St James' Square after the war.
Source: Niece Pauline Myers

Eric Parker Norfolk

Minskip Road.
Army, Catering Corps.
Enlisted early in the war, served in Egypt, then Burma
Source: Son Derek Norfolk

James Tennant

High St.
Army.
Was in the Territorials before the war, enlisted 2nd September 1939, Royal Engineers. First posted to Iceland, then subsequently was in the 8th Army in North Africa and Italy, building bridges.
Source: Sister Jenny (Tennant) Laughey

Henry Tennant

High St.
Army.
Was medically classified C3 (eyes, ears) but still accepted in the Army. Was driver for officers in the RAOC.
Source: Sister Jenny (Tennant) Laughey

Harry Lowther

New Row.
Army.
Source: Jenny (Tenant) (Ingledew) Laughey

Ben Lowther

New Row.
Army.
Source: Jenny (Tenant) (Ingledew) Laughey

Frank Greensitt

High Street, Boroughbridge.

Army.

Enlisted in 1940, trained as a driver in the RASC, and spent the early years of the war on the south coast. Took part later in the preparations for the Normandy invasion transporting ordinance from ammunition dumps to the huge concrete barges in London docks being assembled for the Mulberry Harbour project. Each barge was equipped with an anti aircraft gun, with a magazine underneath which had to be filled with ammunition.

A key part of the preparation for invasion included thoroughly waterproofing the lorries in case they had to be landed in water as they disembarked from the landing craft heading for the beach. This was taken very seriously and thoroughly practiced.

Frank embarked for Normandy 12 days after the D-Day landings. He was able to see the tugs pulling over the Mulberry Harbour concrete barges. Landed at Gold Beach, the water fortunately only as high as the hub caps. The beach was still being shelled by the Germans who were still in control in Caen. Frank thought this was his worst experience of the war. He was attached to an artillery company driving a truck full of shells, on to Bayeux then to Caen. Sometimes he was carrying food and petrol as well as ammunition. As the war progressed he reached Antwerp which was being hit regularly by V2 rockets. Eventually he reached Hamburg and was in Germany on VE day.

However, with the war in the Far East still continuing, Frank began training on amphibious vehicles preparing for moving to the war with Japan, but the dropping of the atomic bomb brought the war to a timely end. Frank was briefly posted to Naples before being demobbed in 1946. After the war he went to live in Preston.

Source: Sheree Livesey

Frank Boddye

Originally from Skelton, lived in New Row immediately after the war.
Army No.14589615 Royal Artillery, 8th Army.

Fought in the invasion of Italy, through Cassino then took part in the Anzio landings fiasco, surviving the blood bath there, January to May 1944. Finished up in Thessaloniki, Greece at the end of the war.

Source: Daughter Pauline Boddye

Aldborough

Bernard Clayton

Joined RAF in 1940. Bomber Pilot flying Wellington, Halifax and Lancaster bomber missions from 1941-1944, completing a remarkable three tours, 82 missions against some of the most dangerous targets in Europe, including Berlin, Hamburg and Turin, though the average life of a bomber crew was five missions.

Had completed two operational tours by June 1943, awarded the DFC, CGM and DSO. Joined the famous 617 Squadron in 1943 after Dam Busters Raid, took part in several specialised and highly dangerous raids. Stood down from active service mid 1944, then trained bomber crews up to end of the war.

Participated in Berlin Airlift in 1948, doing 103 missions transporting vital supplies. Was subsequently test pilot on many new aircraft, but was tragically killed in 1951 as a passenger on a plane that crashed on a test flight.
Source: Niece Judith Clayton

Captain John Clayton

Army, S/N 4393108

Eldest of the Clayton brothers, called up at the beginning of the war into the Green Howard Regiment. Soon sent to France with the British Expeditionary Force, and was one of the lucky ones to be rescued from the beaches of Dunkirk.

Posted to North Africa for the fight against Rommel's Afrika Korps in the desert war. He was awarded the Military Medal for outstanding action under fire in the attack on the heavily defended German defence line in Tunisia at Mareth in March 1943 and the subsequent blood bath at Wadi Akarit, actions won at great cost to the Green Howards.

John was one of the first ashore on D-Day, and he continued the fight through France and Germany until the final capitulation in May 1945.

Source: Niece Judith Clayton, London Gazette (25th November 1943)

Geoff Clayton

Joined RAF in 1944, sent to America for Bomber training, but developed rheumatoid arthritis on return to UK, was grounded and spent the rest of the war on radar.

Source: Niece Judith Clayton

Chapter 4. Active Servicemen Surviving The War — Aldborough

Eric Pratt

4753442 Corporal G E Pratt.

Enlisted 30th May 1940 in York & Lancaster Regiment. After training on Salisbury Plain and Ireland was posted to India via South Africa by sea. In Burma as a foot soldier. Had dental treatment in Bangalore, India in 1943-44, where he must have had respite periods. Like many others suffered from malaria whilst in Burma.
Source: Ruth & Richard Pratt

Billy Pratt

Army, Pioneer Corps attached to Royal Engineers. Injured in action following D-Day and invalided out. Was effectively a cripple for the rest of his life
Source: Ruth Pratt, Mary (Pratt) Robinson

Sapper Herbert Craggs

Royal Engineers, Army no. 14329900

Before the war, from 1925-29, was in West Yorks Territorials along with his elder brothers Clare and Godfrey.

Full enlistment 5th Nov 1942. Served with the 604 Railway Construction Company, Royal Engineers, as a platelayer rebuilding bridges and railroads destroyed by the Japanese, also on some new works in Chittagong (India, now Bangladesh) from 23rd July 1944 to 29th Dec 1944, and 15th-17th March 1945. Was then in Burma 18th March-15th August 1945.

He took many photos whilst in India and Burma, including pictures of Japanese surrendering at the end of the conflict—see example below. These have been incorporated into a really beautiful decorated memorial album by his grandson's mother-in-law.

Source: Geoff Craggs

Clare Craggs

Royal Artillery. Gunner, Anti-Aircraft Coastal Defence. South Coast, North Coast and Northern Ireland.

The photo shows Clare when he was in Territorial Army with his brothers Herbert and Godfrey, 1925-29. Godfrey lost his life in the Lancastria disaster—see casualties.

Ernest Rennison

Son of Mr & Mrs J T Rennison of 8 Greenways, Aldborough.

Served with 50th Northumbrian Division when they stormed the beaches on D-Day. Followed up through Normandy, Belgium and hard fighting in Holland. Finished up in the Essex Regiment in Germany. Awarded certificate of "Outstanding Good Service" signed by Field-Marshall Montgomery.

Ernest Rennison (marked) on patrol in Holland, winter 1945.

Ernest Rennison (right) and mate, with two German prisoners, Holland, winter 1945.

Married Mary Clayton, Arrows Terrace
Source: Step-son David Clayton, Cyril Wright, Geoff Craggs, also newspaper cutting (Knaresborough Post?) enclosed in Boroughbridge Studio Players cuttings book, 1946.

Arthur Rennison

Greenways, Aldborough. Ernest's brother.

Army, Black Watch
Source: son Steve, Cyril Wright.

Henry and Christopher Lawson Tancred

Henry and Christopher were twins.
Sgt Henry in Bomber Command,
Sgt Christopher in Transport Command.
Source: James Lawson Tancred, also mentioned in A E Eaton's book "Two Friends, Two different Hells", about Bernard Clayton.

Captain Bobby Darwin

Kings Royal Rifle Corps, then 43rd then 52nd the Green Jackets. Died 1958 in ?Tripoli.
Lived at Aldborough Hall, one daughter Jennifer, still lives at Aldborough Hall.
Source: James Lawson Tancred and Elizabeth House

Lawrence (Lol) Bowes

Army, 4689472. Kings own Yorkshire Light Infantry.
Captured by Germans in Norway April 1940. Was transported through Norway and Denmark in a cattle truck to a PoW camp in Torun (Thorn) Poland, Stalag XX-A where he spent the next $4\frac{1}{2}$ years alongside some 20,000 other PoWs.

As the Russians advanced from the east in the winter of 1944-45, the Germans were afraid that the camp would be overrun, with the prospect of all the prisoners joining the Russians. The camp was evacuated and the prisoners were subjected to a forced march of some 600 miles to the west over a period of some three months in horrendous conditions. Their clothing was in rags, they were starving, marching up to 30 kilometres per day in the depths of winter often without food or drink, many had dysentery, suffered frostbite and many died on the way. Eventually they were liberated as the allies approached from the west.

After the war Lol was reluctant to talk about his experiences which must have been absolutely dreadful.

Source: Walter Lonsdale, Nancy (Gudgeon) Milne, Aidan Foster

Bill Groves

RAF Ground Crew. Trained in Canada, served in Dishforth.

Married Freda Elsie Barugh in 1940/41.

Source: Daughter Carol (Groves) Metcalfe

Bill Ingledew

Army.

Enlisted in 1942 at 17 years old. Was a mechanic in the RASC.

Took part in the follow up to the Normandy invasion, sustained a shrapnel wound in his leg as he sheltered under a lorry when they came under fire.

Was in Dresden at the end of the war, his daughter Pauline remembers him saying he was appalled at the destruction there.

Source: Daughter Pauline Phillips, wife Jenny (Tennant, Ingledew) Laughey

John (Jack) Ingledew

Army.
Served in Africa.

Source: Niece Pauline Phillips, sister-in-law Jenny (Tennant, Ingledew) Laughey

Langthorpe

Photo: Albert, Dennis and Cyril Hare
Source: Jim and Pat (Hare) Smith

LAC Albert Hare

Spent most of the war in Plymouth, probably on anti-aircraft with RAF Regiment.
Source: May Hare

Dennis Hare

Service no 2012011. Driver. Paratrooper in 1st Airborne Division.

Fought in North Africa, Sicily, Italian campaigns.

Parachuted into Arnhem September 1944, landed in the river but was a strong swimmer and able to swim ashore. Was one of the few lucky ones to escape from the Arnhem disaster.

In Norway following Nazi surrender at the end of the war, involved with clearing mine fields, his best friend was blown up and killed right next to him during this operation, his worst experience of the war.

In Palestine following the European war, confronting the Stern gang in their campaign against British occupation.
Source: Wife May Hare

Cyril Hare

Royal Navy, Gunner.
Initial training at HMS Daedalus, then (probably) aircraft carrier Ark Royal.

Cyril had pleuresy when his ship was in Gibraltar, he was taken ashore to recover. For him it turned out to be a stroke of luck, his ship was torpedoed on its way to Malta and sank in the Mediterranean.
Source: May Hare

Levi Tubby

b1907
Enlisted in Royal Navy when he was 16 to get away from farm labouring. He became an explosives expert and at the outbreak of WW2 he re-joined the RN because of his expertise. He served on the Arctic convoys and also in Scandinavia on bomb disposal. At the end of the war he was awarded the BEM.
Source: Niece Mary Maybourne

Donald Tubby

b1920
Enlisted in Kings Own Yorkshire Light Infantry (KOYLI) aged 16 in 1936 (he told them he was 18). Subsequently transferred to the Military Police.

He was evacuated at Dunkirk and coincidentally the ship which picked up him and his men was the ship aboard which his brother PO Harold Tubby was serving! Later Donald served in North Africa and Egypt.

He married a German widow after the war and continued his army career as a Prison Officer in military prisons.

Ken Needham remembers Donald showing him a pair of German U-boat binoculars
Source: Niece Mary Maybourne

Reg Tubby

b1924

Joined Royal Marines aged 16 in 1940 (he told them he was 18).

He served overseas and was shot and injured off one of the islands near Italy. This affected his hearing and gave him health issues after the war.

Source: Niece Mary Maybourne, also Cyril Wright, Sheila Shepherd and Ken Needham

Stanley Ward

b 25/8/1918, father Daniel Ward. Farmer at Milby.

Army, East Yorkshire Regiment.

Enlisted at Richmond 19th March 1942. Embarked for Egypt from Greenock, Scotland 18th December 1942, arrived 21st January 1943. In Western Desert up to July, then to Sicily 10th July. Wounded at Prima Sola Bridge, Sicily 18th July, taken to field hospital along with other casualties, left for three days waiting his turn for treatment amongst other wounded soldiers. Almost left for dead along with others of his colleagues, but groaned when he was moved. He was taken for treatment and miraculously revived. His right leg had to be amputated, his right hand was badly damaged through bullet wounds, his little finger was amputated. Repatriated to UK, disembarking at Glasgow 18th Nov, hospitalised in Bangus Emergency Hospital, Bracus, West Lothian. Back home in Milby by 24th Nov 1943. In and out of hospitals for several years following, fitted with artificial leg, and had operations to his right arm.

After a long period of recuperation and rehabilitation, returned to farming again in Milby after the war, with an artificial leg. He was naturally right handed but he learned to write left handed, and adapted in many other ways to cope with his disability. Despite his considerable war injuries he successfully ran the farm after the war with the help of his son John until he died in February 1992. A remarkably resilient and determined man.

Source: Son John Ward

Conald "Con" Crosby Lowther

Canal House, Langthorpe Boroughbridge, b10/12/1921.

Army no 14253459.

Enlisted with Green Howards, 06/08/1942, at Richmond.

Trained at Skegness to 11/03/43. Embarked for India 12/03/43 arriving 11/06/43. Transferred to Durham Light Infantry (DLI) 07/08/43. Hospitalised 29/08/43-19/10/43.

Entered Burma theatre of operation 08/04/44. Fought at Kohima with 2nd DLI April 1944. Hospitalised 29/04/44, discharged 27/07/44.

Transferred to Royal Army Ordnance Corps (RAOC) 14/03/45. Again hospitalised, 30/04/45-25/05/45.

Con met his old Boroughbridge friend Bob Horner at the end of the war in Singapore before returning home for demob 19/12/46.

Source: Daughter Janet (Lowther) Bennett

Sgt Sidney Metcalfe

Army, Royal Artillery.

Was in the BEF in France, evacuated from Dunkirk. Told his son Peter that he was picked up by a small boat which was some distance out to sea. He and a colleague could not swim, but after downing half a bottle of whisky, they both made a dash for it and somehow managed to reach the small boat and were taken back to England, returning with absolutely nothing.

Later in the war he saw service in an anti-aircraft unit on the South Coast of England, which was credited with shooting down a German ME109 fighter, seen to crash in flames.

In the army until the end of the war.

Source: Son Peter Metcalfe

W/Sgt Arthur Hawkridge

Army No 7946573, Royal Armoured Corps.

Enlisted 15th Jan 42, into 56th Training Reg. Catterick. Took fitters course at Bovington, Dorset, 1942. Served as vehicle mechanic with Eighth Army in North Africa and Italy (with friend Harold Leake from Skelton). After war up to Feb 1947 in 14/20th Kings Hussars.

Source: Cyril Wright, grandson Oliver Hawkridge, Peter Binns

Sgt Herbert Ridley Waite

Rose Cottage, Milby.
Army No 4351296.

Police War Reserve Constable 26/11/39-15/11/41. Enlisted in East Yorkshire Regiment 09/03/42, same time as Stanley Ward. Was in Military Police, promoted to Sergeant 26/03/44. Served in various locations in the UK for the rest of the war, never abroad.

Source: John Ward, John Shepherd, Peter Metcalfe

Sgt Maurice Foster

Army, York and Lancs Regiment.
Served in Egypt, fought in North Africa with Desert Rats. El Alamein in October 1942, also in Crete. Mentioned in dispatches.
Source: Nephew Aidan Foster

Ernest Foster

Artillery or Royal Engineers or possibly Signals.
Cook, machine gunner and eventually searchlight battery operator, initially in southern England and finally at Kirby Hill.
Source: Nephew Aidan Foster

Alec Wardell

Ure Bank House, Langthorpe.
Royal Navy, Able Seaman.
Initial training HMS Ganges, Norfolk. Served on Destroyer HMS Walpole and HMS Schmeitzer in Far East, Ceylon, also Arctic. His ship hit a mine off hook of Holland and was damaged but did not sink.
Source: Wife Ruth (Stubbs) Wardell

Charlie Lee

Unusually, Charlie served in both the RAF and the Army.

Enlisted in RAF in Feb 1942, volunteered for aircrew, and trained as observer/air gunner.

During a training exercise in Northern Ireland his plane was caught in an air pocket, the rapid descent resulted in Charlie suffering a burst ear drum. Following unsuccessful treatment in St Mary's Hospital in Edinburgh, he was invalided out of the RAF, but in February 1943 he was again called up for the Army.

He was recruited into the Military Police, with initial training in Newton Aycliffe, then posted to the Trossachs, Scotland, guarding ammunition dumps.

Subsequently shipped on RN ship Corfu to India, where he served in Bombay and later Karachi.

Discharged 18th August 1946, a year after the Japanese surrender in August 1945.

Came back on SS Strathnaver, the same ship as Alf Stokes, with whom he became a close friend after the war. Married Joyce Kitching 3/09/50

Source: Interview by author, 11/02/2014

Chapter 4. Active Servicemen Surviving The War				Langthorpe

Sgt Herbert Cooke

Langthorpe, b 1916.

Army, REME (Royal Electrical and Mechanical Engineers).

Before the war he worked in farming. After the Normandy invasions in 1944 he was in France. His daughter remembers him saying he was involved in repairing tanks.

The photos show Bert and a colleague, very happy, looking over a captured V1 "buzz bomb", apparently on Tooting Common. This would have been taken when the allied armies overran the V1 bases in France: the V1s would then have been sent home for detailed examination.
Source: Daughter Evelyn Bowman

Bill Cooke

Army
Source: Cyril Wright/Geoff Craggs

Tommy Schofield

Army, possibly Black Watch.
Had a kilt which he occasionally lent to Aidan Foster
Source: Geoff Craggs/Cyril Wright

Walter Schofield

Army, Kings Royal Rifle Corps.
Source: Ken Needham

Herbert Hartley

Dishforth Road, Langthorpe.
RAF.
Drove "Queen Mary" long articulated lorry for moving crashed aircraft parts.
Had a transport business after the war.
Source: Cyril Wright, daughter Janet

Sgt George William Tew

Sergeant in Paratroopers.
Dropped into Arnhem but broke his leg and was shipped out before the main battle commenced.
Source: Nephew David Harrison, grandson James Harrison

Was enlisted in Boroughbridge Home Guard at the age of 17, before enlistment in the army, his Sergeant was Jim Watson. The meeting place was at the bottom of Back Lane in the upper story of a house adjoining the entrance to the Hall. Marching drill was up and down Back Lane, parades were practiced in a garage or similar building at the back of the Three Arrows Hotel. Rifle shooting practice was at the army camp at Ripon on the Kirby Malzeard road, where there was a large firing range. He remembers night duty at the gravel pit at the top of the hill in Grafton (Marton cum Grafton) when each Home Guardsman had a rifle with five rounds of ammunition - with which they were expected to repel a possible German invasion!

Eddie Morrison

Once when on parade, a visiting officer noticed that Eddie was considerably younger than the rest of the Home Guard, and enquired of Sgt Major Frape whether Eddie was serving legally at his age. The reply was "I won't tell Hitler if you don't", which apparently perfectly satisfied the officer.

In his early life he lived at 17 Eastgate Boroughbridge, but his father was part of a Boroughbridge syndicate which won the Irish Sweepstake about 1930, the proceeds of which enabled him to buy the Anchor Pub, Langthorpe, where Eddie lived until he joined the army in October 1942.

Enlisted in the army in 1942 in the Royal Corps of Signals, Army no 14415149.

Initial training at Catterick, dispatch rider training at Prestatyn, North Wales, following which he found himself on a boat heading for France and the Normandy invasion. Was attached to the 1st heavy regiment Royal Artillery as a dispatch rider. His job involved liaison between the infantry and artillery, following the infantry and reporting back to the artillery the direction where shell fire was required to support the infantry. He was frequently under fire.

He followed up into Belgium and Holland, in particular at Nijmegen. Followed up with the fighting into Germany, remembers passing the town of Belsen where most of his ammunition was passed on to soldiers who had entered the concentration camp at Bergen Belsen. It was used to dispose of some of the worst of the German guards there. Eddie heard the shooting although he did not go into the camp. After the German surrender he was stationed at Sprockhovel, Germany.

He was selected to take part in the victory parade in London, representing the whole army. He was recalled to England, sent to Catterick for special new uniform, then to London to take part in the Victory Parade. The assembly area was in Trafalgar Square amongst tumultuous and excited crowds. Someone in the crowd threw an apple hitting Eddie on the head, which really hurt and made him feel nauseous! Participated in the Victory Parade down the Mall with the salute to King George VI, Eddie observed that the King was wearing make-up, the first time he had seen a man with make-up. (presumably for the cameras).

Returned to Speckhoven in Germany for a further two years where Eddie excelled as an athlete, had army medals for long jump, high jump, and 100 metres. Demobbed in 1947.

Source: Interview with Eddie Morrison, age 92, 20.04.2015

Ken Goodall

Army, Dispatch rider.

Source: Eddie Morrison

Others

So far it has not been possible to find significant additional detail on Arthur Myers' war service, though his name appears on the memorial plaque in Kirby Hill church.

Kirby Hill

Flight Lt Jack Jones

RAF.
Son of a World War I pilot, Jack joined the RAF Volunteer Reserves in 1937, flying Hawker Harts, Westland Whirlwinds, Blenheims and other aircraft. He fully enlisted in the RAF at the start of the war.

He was one of "The Few" who flew in the Battle of Britain in 1940, flying Blenheim fighter bombers and Beaufighters.

He was badly injured returning to Hendon from a mission: unbeknown to Jack, at that time the runway had been scattered with concrete blocks because of the fear of a German invasion. Jack's aircraft crashed into one of them, resulting in serious injuries to his arm and leg. He was out of operations for $2\frac{1}{2}$ years, but recovered and spent the last years of the war flying Mosquitos with 25 Squadron.

Was shot down in Bavaria on the last day of the war by friendly fire from an American ack ack unit which mis-identified his aircraft, shot up both engines resulting in him crash landing. Remarkably he suffered no further injury from this crash.

Took part in the Berlin Airlift after the war, and subsequently flew for many years as a civil pilot, firstly with British South American Airlines, then with BOAC when they took over the airline. When he retired in 1973 he flew gliders almost up to his death in 1997.

Source: Aidan Foster, daughter Jill Butterfield, son Nigel Jones

W. (Bill) Thorpe

Army, captured by Japanese probably in Singapore or Malaya, worked as POW on Burma Railway, tortured by Japanese. Was in very poor health when he returned to England. Took 6 years to recover, but never returned to good health.
Source: Andy Willey/Olive Duck/Jimmy Evans.

Lawrence Thorpe

Eastfield, Kirby Hill. Bill's brother. Army.
Source: Olive Duck

Frank Whiting

Tank Corps. Stationed at Boroughbridge Hall camp 1940. During his stay there, they had one Matilda Tank and two obsolete light tanks. Posted to Egypt in 8th Army desert war. Suffered chest infection, declared unfit and returned to England. Demobbed 1946.

Met his wife Vera Ivory from Kirby Hill at dance in Crown Hotel, lived in Kirby Hill after war.
Source: Phone conversation with Frank (92) and wife Vera (91), 19.10.2013.

Henry Kirby

Army, York and Lancs Regiment. In Burma. Driver. Had malaria.

Chapter 4. Active Servicemen Surviving The War				Kirby Hill

Source: David Barley

Tommy Whiteley

Army, Driver on supplies, probably in RASC. Enlisted 1940, demobbed 1946. France D-Day+1, followed up through Belgium, held up for some time in Antwerp due to German counter-attacks, then on to Germany. After war had finished drove bus for Army football team in Germany.
Source: Stan Whiteley, Greta (Whiteley) Binns.

George Wrightson

Army, Green Howards. Fought with 8th Army in Egypt, took part in battle of El Alamein, Tripoli. Possibly also Sicily and Italy, but not known exactly, he was allowed early release as his wife was very ill.
Source: June Young.

Jack Wrightson

Lived near windmill.

Sgt in Army, possibly physical training Instructor. Photo sent from France.
Source: Son Paul Wrightson.

Alfred Lonsdale

Royal Horse Artillery.

Enlisted at Darlington in the regular army as a 17 year old on 16/09/35. Served in India before the war from 14/09/37 to 03/10/39, then transferred to Egypt at the outbreak of war, and served with the desert army in North Africa from 14/10/39 to 10/09/43. Had a home posting from 11/09/43 to 16/07/44, then posted to India 17/07/44 for the fight against the Japanese in the Burmese campaign.

Details of his service are not yet known, but he would certainly be involved in very significant battles of WW2. The photo shows him in full dress uniform, possibly at his passing out parade after his initial training.

Met his wife-to-be Norah during leave at Woolwich Barracks. They married in September 1946. Norah was a sergeant in the ATS.

Source: Brother Walter Lonsdale, son Graham Lonsdale

Kirby Hill   Chapter 4. Active Servicemen Surviving The War

Pte Ronald "Roy" Peacock

Royal Navy. Letter dated 17th August 1944 from Roy Peacock to Stanley Ward, ends 4538728 Pte Peacock R. Defence Platoon, 50th (n) Division. Also mentioned in letter of 24th June is Leslie Myers, D-Day landings letter is from Dave?, A company East Yorks Regiment.
Source: Cyril Wright, Stella (Peacock) Harland

Sgt Christopher William Harland

RAF.
Regular in the RAF from 1933-1945. Ground crew airframe fitter. Before RAF service, was a trained joiner and undertaker. His son Nick says he did not talk very much about the war.
Source: Geoff Craggs, son Nick Harland

Billy Thirkill

Navy
Source: Aidan Foster, confirmed Vera Whiting

Robert Easton

Army.
Probably served in Far East. Wounded.
Source: Margaret Easton.

Ernest Cooper

Army.

POW of the Japanese for $4\frac{1}{2}$ years.
Released early from forces in very poor health. Often visited George Wrightson who was also released early, for support.
Source: June Young, Alan and Ann Hudson.

Robert Cooper

Army, Coldstream Guards.
Source: Alan & Ann Hudson

Arthur Cooper

Army
Royal Armoured Corps, same regiment as Arthur Hawkridge (p51).
Source: Alan & Ann Hudson

Earnest Leckonby

Army.

Arthur Morgan

RAF Ground Crew

Alan Goodall

Langthorpe
Army. Did part of his military service in Iceland.
Source: Daughter Ann (Goodall) Weinhardt.

58

Langthorpe/Kirby Hill—No Information

The following names are entered on the War memorial in Kirby Hill church, for whom no information has yet been obtained: Thomas Baynes, William Baynes, Oswald Bayley, Harry Bean, Len Caygill, Leslie Goodall, Richard Goodall, George Hall, Ernest Hodge, E. Johnson, Ronald Kelsey, Tom Lothian, Arthur Myers, Ronald Myers, Norman Petts, Alwyn Stephenson, Ronald Smith, Albert Smith, Harry Wilson.

Roecliffe

Corporal Donald Crozier

Royal Marines, 1941-1945.
Training at Lympstone/Woodbury Common, Devon.
Coxwain of a troop carrying Landing Craft on D-Day, thought to have landed on Sword beach.
Source: Brother Johnny and wife Carol Crozier

Major Norman Myers

Leyton Cottage Roecliffe.
In Catering Corps, or perhaps Royal Pioneer Corps, in Egypt.
After demob in 1945 he didn't take to civilian life, rejoined the army and was in Egypt in Suez crisis.
Source: Daughter Mary, Johnny and Carol Crozier

Sgt John Benson

Royal Artillery.
Served with Eighth Army in Egypt, where he met up with Jack Varley.
Married Madge Hawkridge, and worked at Waddingtons woodyard after the war.
Source: Geoff Craggs, Janet Shepherd

Thomas Bendelow

Army, West Yorkshire Regiment.
Served in Belgium towards the end of the war.
Source: Daughter Ann Lee

Jack Atkinson

Army, Black Watch.
Jack was enlisted in 1939 and served in the Orkney Islands, probably defending the huge naval base at Scapa Flow. He was batman to a Roman Catholic priest.
Worked at The Crown at Roecliffe after the war.
Source: Johnny Crozier, and daughter Ann Hudson

George Pratt

Army.
Worked at Roecliffe Brick and Tile Works both before and after the war.
Source: "The Pilmoor, BoroughBridge and Knaresborough Railway" Publication, Patrick Howat

Harry Proctor

Royal Engineers.
Source: Johnny and Carol Crozier

Bill Proctor

Pioneer Corps.
Source: Johnny and Carol Crozier

Cliff Burton

Army, York and Lancaster Regiment. Enlisted 1940.
Initial training Hunmanby Hall, then shipped via South Africa to India, posted to North West Frontier. Late in 1942 as the Germans advanced through southern Russia, they posed the threat of an invasion of India through Afghanistan. The defence of the North West Frontier, in which Cliff took part, was bolstered to counter this threat.
As the tide of war turned against the Germans Cliff was posted to Southern India for intensive and extensive jungle training, following which he was posted to Burma and fought alongside the Ghurkas (see photo). He passed through Kohima after the bloody battle of April 1944, and participated in the tough drive against the suicidal "no surrender" Japanese through Meiktila to Rangoon. The Battle of Sittang Bridge and Pagoda Hill followed, in almost impossible monsoon conditions with many casualties.
The fighting was finally brought to an end with the dropping of the atomic bombs on Hiroshima and Nagasaki.
Returned to England in January 1946. Rarely talked about the war when he returned to England.
Source: Aidan Foster, wife Gwen Burton

Minskip

The memorial pictured below is in Minskip village hall.

Biographical sketches of men in the forces follow. For the women's biographies see Chapter 7, p101, and for Mines see Chapter 12, p119.

N F Denny

Royal Navy
No further information. This may even be a mistaken entry on the war memorial: could refer to W F Denny. This is still being investigated.

Malcolm Raymond Styan

Royal Navy, Stoker.
Enlisted as volunteer before he was 18, training at HMS Devonshire, shore base in Plymouth. Later at sea, his ship was attacked, possibly torpedoed or bombed, he was in the water for 5 hours before rescue. His daughters could not remember the name of his ship.

Demobbed in 1945.
Source: Daughters Audrey (Styan) Horton, Ann (Styan) Sadler

Herbert Allen

Army RASC.
Service in UK, N.Ireland.
Source: Son Frank Allen

Billy Ayres

Army.
Brothers Arthur and Clifford were in the Home Guard, Boroughbridge.
Source: Frank Allen

Herbert Deighton

Prospect Terrace, Minskip.
Army.
Source: Frank Allen

Harry Dodsworth

Army.
Captured by the Italians, was POW in Italy, escaped, was cared for by farmer in Italy after escape. Details not known precisely, but possibly captured either in North Africa or initial invasion of Italy. Escaped at the time of the Italian surrender, and was hidden by partisans from the Germans whilst they were still in Italy.
Source: Daughter Joan (Dodsworth) Lyon, Frank Allen

H. Evans

Army

J. Greensitt

Army

Percy Lambert

Army, Royal Artillery.
Service in UK only.
Source: Son Ken Lambert

Walter Lindsey

Army, West Yorkshire Regiment.
Released shortly after enlistment due to bad feet.
Source: Daughters Mary (Lindsey) Wood, Pauline (Lindsey) Henley

Clarence Scott

Army.
Was a chef at the Three Arrows before and after the war and was also a chef in the army.
Source: Audrey (Styan) Horton

Sgt Donald Mawtus

Army, RASC. Service No. 171558.
Enlisted 04.04.1940. Served first in the Orkney Islands (Scapa Flow?) then posted to Folkestone. Then spent 2 years in Sierra Leone.
Demob 30.04.1946.
Source: Wife Connie Mawtus

Tommy Watts

2, Prospect Terrace
Army, RASC.
Truck driver, in the second wave follow up to the D-Day landings in Normandy. Followed through to the end of the war into Germany. Finished his service in Nuremburg at the time of the War Crimes Trials in 1946, after which he returned to England for demob.
Married Betty Daniel from Roecliffe, lived in Staveley after the war.
Source: Son Vaughan Watts, son-in-law Ron Gargett

Kenny Campbell

RAF
Source: Mary Marsh

Leslie W. Campbell

RAF
Source: Mary Marsh

Henry Horner

RAF

C. Dennis Kirby

Minskip, Born 1926
RAF. Air crew engineer. Service no. 3040156.

Survived the war but was killed in a flying accident during a training exercise aged 23 when two Lincoln bombers collided in mid-air, 26 September 1949. RE374 of No. 57 Squadron RAF and RF407 of No. 61 Squadron RAF collided and crashed over Shropshire; seven on each aircraft were killed. Dennis is buried at Aldborough.

Source: Aidan Foster

Geoff Mawtus

RAF Ground Crew
Aircraft servicing in Lincolnshire.
Source: Sister-in-law Connie Mawtus

Chapter 5
Doug Lofthouse's Photos from Malta

Doug Lofthouse of Boroughbridge (see p19) was an engine fitter with the RAF, stationed on Malta from 1941-43. During this period Malta was the most-bombed place in the world: as a logistics centre for supplying the Allies in the Desert, and a launchpad for the Allies' own successful operations against Axis supplies to North Africa, it was a prime target. So severe was the situation on Malta that the island (including the military) were very close to starvation in 1942. Eventually the entire population was awarded the George Cross, the highest honour available to civilians supporting the war effort: this was the only time in the war that the GC was awarded to a whole population.

Doug took his camera, and was able to take a remarkable variety of photos, often from an aerial vantage point. The following are from his album, assembled at the time or very shortly afterwards. His photos and their laconic captions, taken below directly from Doug's album, are a remarkable reminder of the realities of the war.

Source: Son Mick Lofthouse.

Fighting Through To Malta

Chapter 5. Doug Lofthouse's Photos from Malta

Refuelling At Sea

Escort Plane Shot Down

Chapter 5. Doug Lofthouse's Photos from Malta

Capital Ships Patrol

Ark Royal In Grand Harbour

Chapter 5. Doug Lofthouse's Photos from Malta

Defender L Class

Convoy Attack In Grand Harbour

68

Chapter 5. Doug Lofthouse's Photos from Malta

Destroyer Sinking In Grand Harbour

Relief Ship Bombed

Chapter 5. Doug Lofthouse's Photos from Malta

Luqa Airfield

Landing At Luqa With Blenheim

Chapter 5. Doug Lofthouse's Photos from Malta

Tinge Barracks, Sliema

61 Squadron

Chapter 5. Doug Lofthouse's Photos from Malta

Ship goes up in smoke

Beaufighter service

Chapter 5. Doug Lofthouse's Photos from Malta

Engine Fitter Lofty, Malta

Beaufighter returns from Op

Chapter 5. Doug Lofthouse's Photos from Malta

Beaufighter snag sort out

Beaufighter Test Flight

Chapter 5. Doug Lofthouse's Photos from Malta

Liberator with supplies

Liberator

Chapter 5. Doug Lofthouse's Photos from Malta

Liberator, bomb doors open

Blenheim landing

Chapter 5. Doug Lofthouse's Photos from Malta

Blenheim overshot

Swordfish with torpedo

Chapter 5. Doug Lofthouse's Photos from Malta

Swordfish parked up

Ack Ack over Grand Harbour

Chapter 5. Doug Lofthouse's Photos from Malta

Flares and searchlights

HMS Illustrious bombed

79

Chapter 5. Doug Lofthouse's Photos from Malta

HMS Illustrious bombed 2

HMS Illustrious Ship's Bell

80

Chapter 5. Doug Lofthouse's Photos from Malta

New Spitfire arrives

New Spitfire gone

[Ed: these look like Hurricanes. Doug's captions are striking, even so.]

Chapter 5. Doug Lofthouse's Photos from Malta

Hun attacks Malta

Hun Bomb Drop

Chapter 5. Doug Lofthouse's Photos from Malta

Wellington burns out

Me 109

Chapter 5. Doug Lofthouse's Photos from Malta

Bombed Sunderland Flying Boat 1

Bombed Sunderland Flying Boat 2

Chapter 5. Doug Lofthouse's Photos from Malta

Bombed Sunderland Flying Boat 3

Bombed Sunderland Flying Boat 4

Chapter 5. Doug Lofthouse's Photos from Malta

Another fighter lost

And another

Chapter 5. Doug Lofthouse's Photos from Malta

Hurricane caught on deck

More Spitfires, ready for action

Chapter 5. Doug Lofthouse's Photos from Malta

Ju 87 shot down

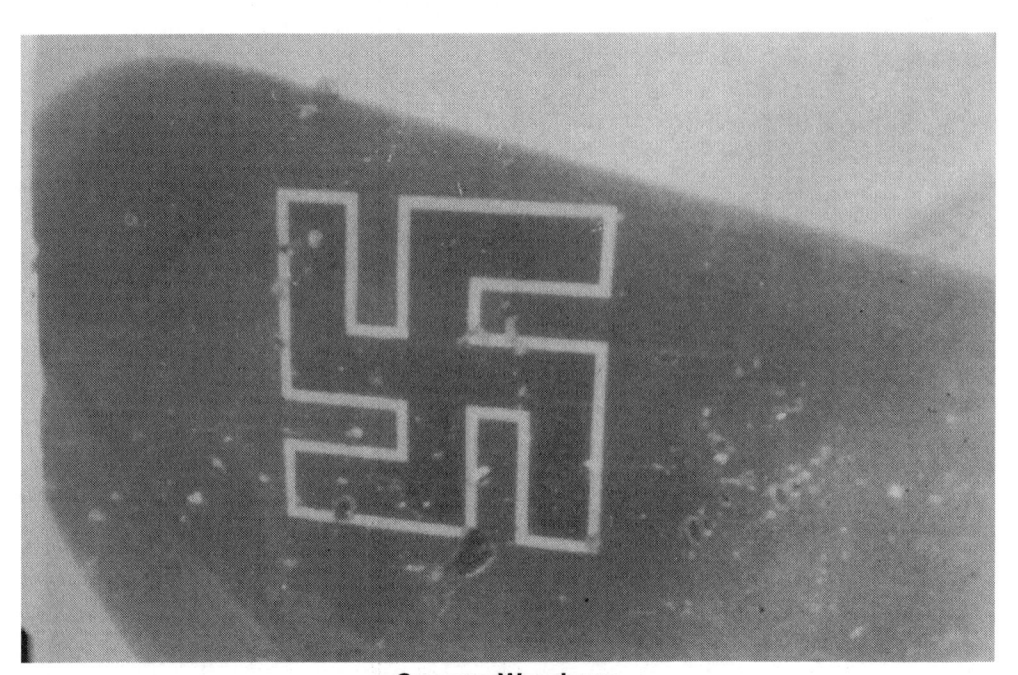

German Wreckage

Chapter 5. Doug Lofthouse's Photos from Malta

Hangers bombed

Hanger Wreckage

89

Chapter 5. Doug Lofthouse's Photos from Malta

Oil Fire

Billet bombed

Chapter 5. Doug Lofthouse's Photos from Malta

Billet bombed again

Billets Wrecked

Chapter 5. Doug Lofthouse's Photos from Malta

More billet wreckage

Remains of showers

Chapter 5. Doug Lofthouse's Photos from Malta

Bombed NAAFI

Bombed MT Yard, LUQA

Chapter 5. Doug Lofthouse's Photos from Malta

Bombed out

Reservoir bombed

94

Chapter 5. Doug Lofthouse's Photos from Malta

New home, Tent

Bombed out but HAPPY

95

Chapter 5. Doug Lofthouse's Photos from Malta

Food running out

Tomato Sustenance

96

Chapter 6
The Royal Canadian Air Force in Boroughbridge

The headquarters for 6 Group Royal Canadian Air Force was at Allerton Castle, and Dishforth was one of the aerodromes used by the Canadians during the war.

425 (Alouette) squadron and 426 (Thunderbird) squadron flew Wellington bombers in operations over Europe from June 1942 to June 1944. The runway was then extended to take heavier bombers, and was used subsequently by the RCAF as a Heavy Conversion Unit (1664HCU) to train crews to fly the Halifax heavy bombers, through to the end of the war.

Many Canadians were accommodated in Boroughbridge from 1942 onwards, amongst them many French Canadians. They were billeted in the Crown, Three Horse Shoes, Three Greyhounds Hotels and other accommodation in the town. Along with the soldiers from the army camp, they were ever-present in the daily life of wartime Boroughbridge. They regularly frequented the pubs in Boroughbridge, the Black Bull being amongst the favourites. Several local girls ended up marrying Canadian airmen.

The author's most vivid and enduring memory of the war was the Canadian airmen climbing up the Fountain to place a maple leaf memorial on the roof (see p165).

Barbara Breckon recalls Marcel, an RCAF lodger who was her brother's godfather, but was later killed in action (see p167).

Jack Lebert's photos

Jack Lebert was a French Canadian airman who married Eileen Robshaw after the war. These photos, kindly provided by Eileen who still lives in Canada, give an impression of RCAF life at Dishforth airbase and in the town of Boroughbridge.

RCAF ground crew squad, Jack Lebert noted with X.

RCAF Dishforth searchlight crew: Marcel "Punchy" Carrier, Jack "Al" Lebert, Jim Bennet, Tommy "Tomcat" Thompson.

Jack Lebert's photos — Chapter 6. The Royal Canadian Air Force in Boroughbridge

On the wing of a USAAF heavy bomber. The USAAF was not stationed at Dishforth, so this visit was probably out of necessity, and must have created some excitement.

Runway control tower. One key role of the controllers was to turn runway landing lights on at night when needed by incoming planes. As soon as possible after landing, they were switched off again as part of the blackout.

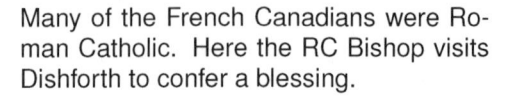

Many of the French Canadians were Roman Catholic. Here the RC Bishop visits Dishforth to confer a blessing.

Clearing snow from the runway.

Memories of Boroughbridge—where else, but by the fountain? ...

Chapter 6. The Royal Canadian Air Force in Boroughbridge — Brief sketches

... or the Black Bull ...

... or even the Midland Bank!

Brief sketches

There can be no claim to be comprehensive in the sketches below. Naturally they tend to come from airmen who married local girls and so established a traceable contact with the town.

Cpl Alphonse Jack Lebert

French Canadian. RCAF, ground crew, stationed at Dishforth.

Involved in airfield and runway maintenance. Also part of a searchlight team.

He met Eileen Robshaw from Arrows Terrace at a dance at the Crown Hotel. They married at the Roman Catholic church in Thirsk on 14th July 1945, and returned to live in Canada after the war.

Source: Wife Eileen Lebert

Ray Leboeuf

French Canadian, RCAF, aircrew, stationed at Linton-on-Ouse.

Cousin to Jack Lebert. They used to meet up often in the pubs in Boroughbridge.

His bomber was shot down towards the end of the war, he was taken prisoner by the Germans, released when the war was over and returned to Canada.

Warrant Officer Neil Peleshok

Ground crew, RCAF, stationed at Dishforth.

Originally from Ukraine, moved to Canada before the war, was a Newfoundland lumberjack. Married Ann Smith, Jim Smith's sister, during the war. Afterwards returned to Canada.

Source: Ruth & Derek Wardell, also Jim Smith.

Joan Holmes

From Bridlington.
WAAF.
Joan travelled through Boroughbridge on her way from Bridlington and visited the town from time to time.

She was a transport driver at Dishforth during 1942, involved primarily with Thunderbird Squadron of the RCAF. Amongst other vehicles she drove a Davy Brown tractor towing aircraft in and out of hangers and to dispersal points, ready for take-off. She transported bombs to the aircraft, and crews too. Any job requiring transport driving she would do.

Accommodation for the WAAFs was in Nissen huts, well separated from the airmen's quarters. There was a NAAFI run by the Salvation army just inside the gates. Dances in the Sergeant's Mess were very popular with the station WAAFS.

When Thunderbird squadron moved to Linton-on Ouse in summer 1943, Joan moved with them and remained with them there until the end of the war.

After the war Joan became a member of the 426 Squadron Thunderbird Association, which holds a memorial day annually, usually in May, at Dishforth. They have a short memorial service and lay a wreath at the church/village hall. Joan organised this event for several years.

Source: Joan (Holmes) Coppack, son Gary Coppack

Chapter 7
Women in the forces

In spring 1941 all women aged 18-60 were required to register with the government for war service. Some—especially single women aged 20-30—were conscripted into the forces.

The women's forces paralleled the men's: the army (ATS, Auxiliary Territorial Service), navy (WRNS, Women's Royal Naval Service) and air force (WAAF, Women's Auxiliary Air Force). The services gave women (as they did also to men) unprecedented mobility, and many married men they met in the forces far from Boroughbridge.

Betty Wardley

New Row, Boroughbridge.
WRNS
Later Elizabeth Elgin, author.

Sgt Olive Duck

Kirby Hill. b 1922.

ATS

Olive worked at Morten's Bakery in Boroughbridge before being called up in 1941. Initial army training was in Newcastle. The following quotes verbatim from *The Life of Olive Duck*, by her great niece Eireann Quinn, aged 12:

"She was posted to Aldershot Bakery, where she baked bread and rolls for the soldiers. When the bakery was making bread they made up a big mixture, then divided it up into loaves. For example one mixing made around about 300 loaves, and they made about 70 mixings per shift. So that's 21,000 loaves per shift.

This is what they put in the mixing; 4 bags flour, 9lb salt, $4\frac{1}{2}$ lbs yeast, 32 gallons of water. It wasn't long before she was made a sergeant and got her stripes.

Chapter 7. Women in the forces

When the then Princess Royal (Queen Elizabeth's sister) visited the bakery, Olive showed her round (see photo).

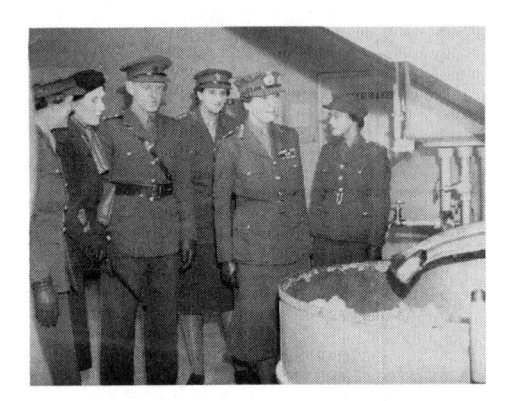

When she was in the war she also saw the mess that the air raids and the blitz made in London.
She made lots of friends when she was there and still keeps in touch with the ones who are still living."
Olive told the present author that in a typical day in the Morten's bakery she would make 200 loaves of bread. The change to 21,000 a shift in the army is an example of the industrialization that characterized the conflict.
Source: "The Life Of Olive Duck" op cit; interview with author May 2014.

Isabelle (Belle) Clayton

Arrows Terrace, Boroughbridge.
ATS (Auxiliary Territorial Service).

Enlisted 20/08/43. Was in HAA (Heavy Anti-Aircraft) Regiment, Royal Artillery. Served on Canvey Island and Thorpe Bay on the north Thames Estuary. Released 30/06/45.
Source: Sister Kath (Clayton) Proctor

May Tubby

Langthorpe
ATS
Served in Morecambe at an underground ammunition depot. Discharged in 1941 when she married.

Emily Robinson

Daughter of Ernest Robinson. High St, Boroughbridge.
WRNS, Naval Officer, catering division

Betty Tilburn

Arrows Terrace, Boroughbridge
ATS
Married soldier Bill Harris, a dock worker from London. They had two daughters Sandra and Pat and a son Brian. Sandra married Harry Redknapp, Pat married Frank Lampard senior, footballers with West Ham United.
Betty's brother was George Tilburn RAF, killed in action over Holland (see p12).
Source: Gwenneth Robson, Ruth (Spearman) Barley. Garry Tilburn

Joan Davy

Fishergate, Boroughbridge.
ATS.
Married Bernard Harcourt, sergeant in army at Boroughbridge, and bandsman.

Joan Ward

Minskip
ATS
Married Harry Thompson, Army, whom she met while in the forces. Harry was involved in the siege of Tobruk.
Source: Cyril Wright

Chapter 7. Women in the forces

Annie Hawkridge

Anchor Terrace.
ATS
After the war, married Jeffrey Harris, Army, Burma
Source: Cyril Wright/Olive Duck/Janet Shepherd

Sgt June Dockray

Daughter of Mr & Mrs F M Dockray, of the Three Greyhounds Hotel, Boroughbridge.

WAAF, served four years, as a training officer at Beaulieu Camp (a special operations training centre).

After the war, married Stan Burley.
Source: Son Mike Burley, contemporary newspaper cutting

Barbara Taylor

Boroughbridge.
WAAF. Was involved in navigation (perhaps radar?) for anti aircraft guns at Spurn Head. Hull was the most heavily bombed city in the UK during the war.
Married Eric Watson.
Source: Son Mike Watson, neice Chris (Murdoch) Sillman

Mary Olive Perris

Greenways, Boroughbridge.
WAAF.
After the war, married Jim Petty.
Source: Maureen Deignan, Margaret Chandler

Gladys Derbyshire

Kirby Hill
ATS
Source: Vera Whiting

Violet Watts

Sister of Eric Watts.
ATS
Source: Gwenneth (Robshaw) Bird

Ruth Dagget

Daughter of Dr Dagget, Kirby Hill.
ATS, driver.

Lillian Malton

Kirby Hill
ATS

Chapter 7. Women in the forces

Vera Baynes
Kirby Hill
ATS

Vera Waddington
Kirby Hill
ATS

Margaret Waddington
Kirby Hill
ATS

Bernice Farrar
New Row, Boroughbridge.
ATS
Source: Ruth (Spearman) Barley, confirmed sister-in-law Muriel Farrar

Sheila Wardell
Sister of Alec Wardell
ATS

Winnie Richardson
ATS

Barbara Gault
Springfield Road, Boroughbridge.
WRNS

Olive Gault
Springfield Road, Boroughbridge.
WRNS

Dorothy Burley
High St, Boroughbridge.
WRNS
Source: Cyril Wright

Joan Eagle
WAAF

Barbara Wilkinson
Kirby Hill
WAAF

Betty Daniel
Roecliffe. WAAF.
Driver. Stationed at Spitalgate airfield near Grantham. Was an auxiliary driver, drove trucks, staff cars and other vehicles. Later posted to Bangor, Wales.
Married Tommy Watts, lived in Staveley.
Source: Vaughan Watts, Ron Gargett

Chapter 7. Women in the forces

Jean Ligertwood

Minskip Lodge.
ATS.
Served six years with the Motor Transport Companies, rising to the rank of subaltern.
Married Lieut. Col. Horace Claude Benson of Whixley in 1947, a doctor and ex-POW of the Japanese who had worked on the Burma railway.
Source: Boroughbridge Studio Players scrap book

Edna Campbell

WAAF.
Source: Mary Marsh

Evelyn Watts

Roecliffe Lane, Boroughbridge.
WRNS.
Married a paratrooper who she met whilst in the forces.
Source: Joyce (Robshaw) Parkinson

Viera Watts

Roecliffe Lane, Boroughbridge.
ATS.
Evelyn's sister.
Source: Joyce (Robshaw) Parkinson

Joyce Robshaw

Arrows Terrace, Boroughbridge.
ATS.
Younger sister of Jack Robshaw (p38) and Eileen Robshaw (p115).
Volunteered for the ATS on her 18th birthday, just one week before the Japanese surrender on August 15th 1945. Served 18 months in the ATS.
Married a Flying Officer who she met whilst in the forces.
Source: Joyce (Robshaw) Parkinson

105

Chapter 7. Women in the forces

Chapter 8
Searchlight Batteries

There were Searchlight Batteries at Kirby Hill (near the church), Milby (on the road to Helperby), Aldborough (Dunsforth Road) and Roecliffe (on Bishop Monkton side). These were manned by the army, and were undoubtedly for the purpose of protecting Dishforth Airfield.

While in the army, Ernest Foster worked on the searchlight battery at Kirby Hill.
Source: Aidan Foster

Fred Thatcher , Army, from London, also worked on the Kirby Hill Battery. He married Ann Lonsdale from Aldborough. They lived in London after the war.
Source: Walter Lonsdale

Chapter 8. Searchlight Batteries

Chapter 9
Prisoners of War

There were many prisoners of war in the Boroughbridge area, initially Italians, then later Germans.

The author remembers seeing an army truck full of chattering Italian POWs passing the recreation field (The Rec) on the Great North Road near Eastgate.

German PoWs had been accommodated in the old brewery in Langthorpe which later became a laundry. Chris Thompson, who was responsible for clearing the premises when the laundry was closed down, had known since his childhood that PoWs had been accommodated there. He remembers finding a number of swastikas painted on the walls in one of the rooms. He thought it would have been big enough to accommodate about 20 PoWs.

Some PoWs were camped temporarily in the Nissen huts adjoining Springfield Road. There were some 400 German PoWs at Dishforth, some in the old workhouse at Ouseburn. Some of these worked on the local farms, some were known to help with the erection of the Dorman Long temporary bridge after the collapse of the old stone bridge in July 1945 (see p 153).

Horst Weinhardt

After the war some elected to stay in England, one of these was Horst Weinhardt.

Horst was enlisted in the German Navy, serving in U-boats. In the war he suffered being depth charged twice, but survived both, was picked up the second time by the Royal Navy and taken prisoner, initially in a PoW camp at Leithley, near Otley.

He worked as a PoW on Harold Hawking's farm at Ellenthorpe (later J C Lister's), then after the war, decided to stay in England, and continued to work on Lister's farm for the next 38 years. He married a local girl, and had two sons and one daughter.

When he retired his son wanted to take him out for the day, they went to a motorcycle event at Hutton Conyers, where a motorcycle went out of control at high speed and crashed into the crowd: Horst was killed. So ironic, after surviving twice being depth charged in World War II to end life in this way.

Source: Daughter-in-law Ann Weinhardt

Chapter 9. Prisoners of War

Chapter 10

Local Civilians Working For The Military

Lifeboat building at the John Boddy Woodyard

The Boddy family boat building business had been started well before the war, initially in their New Row workshop as early as 1932. In those early days lifeboats were transported down High Street to the Railway Goods Yard on a horse drawn bogey, then on to the customer by rail. Subsequently in 1934 John Boddy bought land in Valuation Lane with direct access to the River Ure and established his workshop there. He built both leisure cruisers and lifeboats, his clinker built boats were well suited for either.

As the war started John's boat building skills were urgently needed for building lifeboats, essential equipment in view of the dreadful loss of British shipping to U-boats in the Battle of the Atlantic. He was therefore exempted from military service, and over 100 lifeboats for the Navy were made at the woodyard on Valuation Lane during the war, probably for both the Royal Navy and the merchant navy.

Boat-building workshop

Boddy's 100th lifeboat

Fire control boats, ie boats equipped with fire hose were also made at the woodyard. Ports were heavily bombed during the war and fires in dockside warehouses were frequent. Boddy's fire control boats would be on hand to tackle these dockside fires.

Lifeboat on a railway bogey

A Boddy's fireboat

Source: Frank Boddy junior

Homing Pigeons

Pigeon racing was active in Boroughbridge well before the war, Jimmy Boyle and Tommy Dodsworth from New Row were leading personalities, also John Ellis and Harry Turner from Aldborough.

When war broke out, pigeon racing was not allowed, but homing pigeons were highly valued as messenger carriers. The War Ministry provided special bakelite cages with corn feeding boxes, for transporting the pigeons, particularly in aircraft. They were used in the bombers flying from Dishforth. In the event of a bomber having to ditch in the sea or make a forced landing whilst on a mission, the homing pigeon could be released with a message giving the location of the aircraft, offering the crew the possibility of rescue.

Jimmy Boyle

Pigeon cage

Jimmy Boyle was the area coordinator, and through him the pigeons in their special cages would be passed on to a contact at Dishforth for use on aircraft. Messages which came back were passed on through the police station—conveniently on the other side of New Row!—to the appropriate contact at Dishforth.

His son Michael has one of the special metal message containers which was strapped to the pigeon's leg.

The author remembers seeing the pigeons flying around Jimmy's pigeon loft, completely oblivious of the contribution they were making to the war effort. They were well in view from the gardens at the backs of New Row.

Source: Michael Wilson, Michael Boyle

Dishforth Aerodrome

A number of civilian workers were employed by the Department of Works, particularly at Dishforth. For example, Walter Seaman from New Row, Boroughbridge, worked as a civilian engineer at Dishforth throughout the war.

Civilian workers at Dishforth at the conclusion of hostilities in 1945
Source: Barbara (Seaman) Breckon

Aircraft manufacture

Billy Capstick, of New Row, was a joiner before the war, and was sent to work at factories in Brough and Sherburn-in-Elmet as a joiner, manufacturing Fairey Swordfish and other wood-framed aircraft.

Source: Michael Wilson

Submarine painting

Having served in the Boroughbridge ARP until April 1942, Herbert Tasker was then drafted for work on Submarines at the Vickers Armstrong Ship Building and Repair works at Walker on Tyne, Newcastle. As a skilled painter and decorator, the job he was allocated was painting parts of the insides of submarines with luminous paint. It must have involved painting special equipment as occasionally he was able to cover no more than one square yard of paintwork a day.

He was released from this work in December 1944 and put in charge of painting work at Dishforth Aerodrome to the end of the war. There he was in charge of German POWs helping with painting work.

Source: Sons Colin and Mike Tasker

Chapter 11
Women in war work

In spring 1941 all women aged 18-60 were required to register with the government for war service.

Women in the forces are covered in Chapter 7. Women with young children were considered to have pressing home duties. Others were required to do war work, especially munitions factories.

The main civilian employers of women from Boroughbridge were the Greenwood and Batley bullet and shell factory in Farnham, just north of Knaresborough, and the Royal Ordnance Factory at Thorp Arch, near Wetherby (see map, p5). Cora Hammond's story below gives a vivid impression of life in the factories, along with the daily commute.

An alternative was the Land Army, in which women provided extra agricultural labour, and could have been posted far from home.

Greenwood & Batley Bullet and Shell Factory, Farnham

Source: The factory name was confirmed by Kathleen (Lumsden) Busby who worked at Greenwood & Batley after the war.

Cora (Herron) Hammond

Boroughbridge. b 01/01/1925.

When she was $17\frac{1}{2}$ in 1942 Cora was conscripted to work at Greenwood & Batley's.

She would leave Boroughbridge square at 7.20am on a Jack Dodsworth work bus, arriving at the Farnham factory to start work at 7.45am. The bus was full of women from Boroughbridge and Minskip. Work was compulsory 12 hour shifts from Monday to Friday and half day Saturday morning. The workforce was almost entirely women as the menfolk were away in the war. Busloads of women arrived from Knaresborough and Harrogate, their numbers must have been quite considerable.

Special clothing was provided for handling the inflammable materials, so on arrival, they changed into rubber shoes, overalls, and hair covering. Cigarettes were obviously banned in the factory, and there were inspectors there checking.

The factory was divided up into bays as a fire risk precaution. There was a loading machine to put cordite into the shell cases and separately, a measured amount of powder. A "needle" machine was used to compress the powder in a special bay. This could be a dangerous operation as occasionally the powder would ignite and flash over. The powder was sealed, and the half-loaded shell cases transported to another factory in Leeds to have the bullet/cannon shells inserted.

Cora remembers a fire one day when one of the women had sneaked her cigarettes through security, she lit up and, bingo!, the powder between the floorboards ignited. Everyone dashed for the door to get outside, fortunately no one was injured.

As the work tailed off towards the end of the war, Cora joined the Civil Service in Harrogate. She married William Hammond (RAF Dishforth) at St James' Church in 1947.

Source: interview with Cora, 24/09/2013. Cora also provided the majority of the names below, women from Boroughbridge on the bus to and from Farnham.

Eileen Robshaw

Married French Canadian from RAF Dishforth. Went to live in Canada.

Mavis Leeming

Roecliffe Road

Winnie Herron

Edna Hughes

Cora's sister. She had to work, her husband George Hughes was a prisoner of war (see p34).

Winnie Rabbit

Minskip.

Mary Clayton

Arrows Terrace.

Chrissie Thompson

Married Ken Clayton.

Madge Hawkridge

(As noted below, Madge also worked at Thorp Arch. It would not have been surprising for one woman to work in two different places during the four years in which war work was compulsory.)
Source: Cyril Wright

Jenny Kirby

Kirby Hill

Jenny Reed

Eastgate
Source: Julia Calley

Vera McKellah

Arrows Terrace. Married Jack Burks (p37).

Source: Son Ross Burks

Janet Atkinson

Lodged with George Wright, married a pilot, Don Turner

Kath Edwards

Kirby Hill. Married Canadian airman.

Gladys Waite

Langthorpe. Married Sidney Metcalfe.

Freda Elsie Barugh

Aldborough. Married Bill Groves.

Audrey Styan

Minskip.

Thorp Arch Munitions Factory

At its peak the Thorp Arch munitions factory employed 18,000 people, mostly women, working round the clock in three shifts. It was serviced by its own railway which dropped off workers, mostly from Leeds and York, at four points around the factory site. Boroughbridge workers travelled in and out by bus.

Lill Hudson

Aldborough. Filled shells and bombs with TNT. Married Maurice Stott from Springfield Road.
Source: Cyril Wright

Eleanor Chipchase

Boroughbridge
Source: Cyril Wright

Betty Mudd

Boroughbridge

Chapter 11. Women in war work
Land Army

Source: Dorothy (Mudd) Coleman

Madge Hawkridge

(As noted above, Madge also worked at Farnham.)
Boroughbridge

Ellen Atkinson

Eastgate, Boroughbridge. Paddy Atkinson's wife.

Land Army

Phyllis Waite

Langthorpe. Worked for Waddingtons on Forestry.

Stella Peacock

Kirby Hill

Freda Stubbs

Worked in Devon

Source: Sister Ruth Wardell

Jenny Tennant

High Street, Boroughbridge.
Drafted for war work when she was 18, worked in Kelly's Cafe, Stump Cross, Boroughbridge.
This transport cafe was used as a catering establishment attached to the NAAFI, for troops on manoeuvres and in transit. She stayed on at Kelly's after the war, where she met her future husband Bill Ingledew, who worked at the petrol station there after demob from the army.
Source: Jenny (Tennant, Ingledew) Laughey

Violet Taylor

St James's Square, Boroughbridge.
From 1939 to 1942 Violet was a Red Cross Nurse initially in St Thomas Hospital in London, moved to St Peter's at Botley Park when the blitz began.
Married Don Murdoch in 1942.
Source: Daughter Christine (Murdoch) Sillman

Chapter 12
Bevin Boys

Coal was a vital commodity as a fuel for the war industry, not least also for domestic use. Coal mining was therefore a reserved occupation. Even so, there was a shortage of miners to produce the quantity of coal needed, and some men—about 48,000 in total—were therefore conscripted as coal miners rather than being called up for the armed forces. The program launched by Ernest Bevin, the Minister for Labour and National Service, and the nickname "Bevin Boys" inevitably followed.

Bevin Boys from Boroughbridge and around included
- Stan Burley
- Tom Gudgeon (Marton cum Grafton)
- Fred Kirby (Aldborough)
- Lawrence Helm (Aldborough)
- Roy Pearson (Aldborough)
- A. Greensitt (Minskip)

Source: Cyril Wright, Ruth Pratt (nee Kirby), Geoff Craggs, Minskip War Memorial

Chapter 12. Bevin Boys

Part II

The Services In Boroughbridge

Chapter 13
Home Guard

The Home Guard, (initially the Local Defence Force) consisted of local volunteers ineligible to join the army because of age, either too old or too young, or in reserved occupation such as farming. At the start of the war, there was a real danger of invasion by German paratroops.

The Boroughbridge unit was lead by Harold Frape, a veteran from World War I, and school headmaster. North of the river, a separate unit operated at Kirby Hill.

The local Home Guard units were constituted under the 14th West Riding Battalion, Home Guard.

A member of the Boroughbridge Home Guard was Eddie Morrison (p54) who remembers details of its early operations. The meeting place was at the bottom of Back Lane in the upper story of the house which had been the old Police Station, adjoining the entrance to Boroughbridge Hall. Marching drill was up and down Back Lane, parades were practiced in a garage or similar building at the back of the Three Arrows Hotel. Rifle shooting practice was at the army camp at Ripon on the Kirby Malzeard road, where there was a large firing range. Eddy remembers night duty at the gravel pit at the top of the hill in Grafton (Marton cum Grafton) when each Home Guardsman had a rifle with five rounds of ammunition - with which they were expected to repel a possible German invasion!

Boroughbridge

Source:

Boroughbridge　　　　　　　　　　　　　　　　　　　Chapter 13. Home Guard

Julie Frape

The photo shows the Boroughbridge Home Guard marching along York Road, followed by the Fire Service. The Parade is leaving St James's Square, the Black Bull pub can be seen in the background. Harold Frape is saluting. The commanding officer taking the salute may be Major Holiday. Behind the wall on the right hand side is the army camp. It is just possible to see a Nissen hut, others are hidden by the trees.

Known members of the Boroughbridge Home Guard include:

- Regimental Sergeant Major Harold Frape
- Sergeant Bob Pinkney
- Sergeant Jim Watson
- Ken Clayton (Aldborough)
- Billy Steel
- Sergeant Arthur Gudgeon (Aldborough)
- Bill Norfolk (Aldborough)
- Eric Craggs (Aldborough)
- Bob Lofthouse
- Bill Cundall (Minskip)
- Raymond Abbott (Marton cum Grafton)
- Corporal ? Hunter
- Charlie Wigby (Roecliffe)
- ? George Ward (Milby)
- Dodge Bailes (Aldborough)
- Frank Lonsdale (Aldborough)
- Les Bowes (Aldborough)
- Joe Taylor (Aldborough)
- Arthur Clayton (Langthorpe)
- Eddie Morrison (Langthorpe)
- Arthur Ayres (Minskip)
- Clifford Ayres (Minskip)

Bob Pinkney　　　Arthur Gudgeon

One Home Guard meeting place was a caravan on Grafton Road just off York Road cross roads. Arthur Gudgeon's wife used to clean it.

In one mock battle Eric Craggs was "captured", and unceremoniously dumped in the "Nanny Pit"—an old quarry just off the York Road.

Source: Phone Interview with Eric Gudgeon

Chapter 13. Home Guard   Kirby Hill

Kirby Hill

Source: unknown

Kirby Hill, which was in the North Riding, being north of the river Ure, had its own Home Guard unit. In addition to those shown on the above photo, members included:

- Sergeant Johnny Graham (of the Canal Garage)
- Douglas Green
- Herbert Foster
- Harry Cooper
- Leslie Styan
- Lance Styan
- Willie Thirkill
- Ossie Barley

Source: Aidan Foster

Another local unit operated at Staveley under Major Holiday.

Chapter 14
Royal Observer Corps

Source:
Ruth (Norris) Bispham

The role of the ROC was to report sightings of enemy aircraft as part of the coordinated National Air Defence organisation. In 1940-41, with the threat of airborne invasion, they also had to be alert to the possibility of German paratroop landings.

The local ROC, station S2, operated from an underground bunker and platform just past the Windmill at Kirby Hill. It was ideally positioned to give an excellent view over Dishforth airfield and the surrounding area. They operated on a 4 hours on 8 hours off shift basis.

ROC Members:

- Oliver Norris (Staveley)
- George Wright (High Street)
- Tom Cousins (Shop Manager, Moss's shop in High Street)
- Mr Walton (Grocery shop, High street)
- Ron Howgate (Kirby Hill)
- Leo Tessyman
- Arthur Whitaker
- Eddy Edwards
- Others

Source: Cyril Wright (who used to deliver coal to them)

Chapter 14. Royal Observer Corps

Source: Ruth (Norris) Bispham

Tom Cousins, George Wright, Ronald Howgate, Mr Walton(?), Leo Tessyman, Oliver Norris, Arthur Whitaker, Eddy Edwards.

Chapter 15
Air Raid Precautions

The remit of the ARP nationally was to ensure the local civilian population was well prepared for the effects of air attacks and (in conjunction with other emergency services such as the police, fire and medical services) to deal with the consequences of such raids. They were responsible for the distribution of gas masks in the early stages of the war and the enforcement of the black-out throughout the war period.

The ARP organisation was established in Boroughbridge at the outbreak of war, their first meeting was held on 5th September 1939. A rota was organised for one warden to stand by in readiness for air raid warnings each night in Deputy Head Warden Herbert Tasker's house in New Row, where a telephone existed to liaise with other organisations involved with the war effort. A log book was started to record all relevant events.

Early wardens were Arthur Linfoot, Arthur Buck, Maurice Calvert, Sid Pullan, E Burley, Paul Armstrong, Frank J Hind, Ronnie Topham, and George Mudd.

Herbert Tasker in gas-protective clothing

Wardens were all issued with uniforms, and the air raid siren was installed in the Police Station on 6th November 1939. Black-out patrols were instituted and gas masks were distributed to the local populace. Training for wardens was given on reporting procedures, aircraft recognition, first aid, rescue procedures, fire fighting, gas attack procedures etc.

In the early years of the war the records show passing enemy raiders. Enemy activity in the area was at its height in the early months of 1941 when several bombing incidents were recorded. The people of Boroughbridge certainly needed no reminder that there was a war on.

Some ARP log book entries:

25.4.41 (date of raid on Linton airfield): 2 sticks bombs dropped, all windows & doors shook approx 23.05. R Kettlewell, 23.05.

5.5.41: Wardens on duty Paul, Burley, Pullan, Buck, AFL, (Linfoot), Hind. 3 bombs dropped westward direction, 00.09. 4 bombs dropped westward direction, 00.10. Watson S/C462 2.50(am); C?.Hope S/C 451; W.Waddington S/L SC.

12.5.41: Wardens on duty Burley, AFL (Linfoot) Buck, Hind, Topham, Mudd, Kettlewell, Paul, Pullan. Heavy gun fire due east 01.04, supplementary fire parties standing by. Bombs dropped 01.38. Watson S/C462 2.50(am); Hope S/C 451.

Chapter 15. Air Raid Precautions

Chapter 16
Fire Service

Personnel 1940-41 (left to right in photo):

- Jim Preston (Market Trader)
- Sid Smith (Butcher - now Greenwoods)
- Guy Willey (father of Andrew, 31 years a fireman, Station Officer 1954 - 1971)
- Cyril Holmes (?)
- Cam Watson (Father of George and Eric)
- Earnest Shipley (Plumber, worked for Jim Petty)
- Jim Petty (Plumber)
- Arthur Leeming (?)
- Walter Dinsdale (long serving on Nidderdale Council)

Source: Andrew Willey

Chapter 16. Fire Service

Fire Practice, High St, 1942
Source: Pat (Leeming) Rowntree

Chapter 17
Police and Special Constables

PC A Blacklock (Boroughbridge), PC Jim Harley (Aldborough) were the civilian policemen with all the usual responsibilities that implies.

Special Constables had additional responsibilities. One responsibility was to convey the government's instruction, in the case of an enemy invasion, for all vehicle owners to immobilize their vehicles by "removing distributor head and leads, and emptying the tank or removing the carburettor", so as to deny them to the enemy.

Police and SPCs
Back Row: Ernest Hope, Earnest Shipley?, Harold Orr, ?, ?, ?, (slightly in front) ?, Wilf Nicholson (Aldborough)
3rd Row: ?, ?, ?, Daniel Clift, ?, ?, ?, ?
2nd row: ?, ?, Harold Akers, ?, PC Blacklock?, Johnny Pickering, ?, ?,
Front row: Mr Morten (cake shop), Jack Reed, Hubert Pullan, ?, ?, Herbert Wardley
Source: Sandra Clift, Elaine Porter

Chapter 17. Police and Special Constables

Chapter 18
Civilian Ambulance Service

Ambulance crew
?, Jack Boddy, ?, Ethel Hope (driver), (on tailboard) Elizabeth "Molly" Boddy, Ivy (Busby) Cundall, ?
Source: Frank Boddy, Elaine Porter

Chapter 18. Civilian Ambulance Service

Nursing staff
Back row: Mary Smailes, Jean Rae, Mrs Gibson, Mrs Pearce; Front row: Betty Winder, Julia Reynard, ?, Ivy (Busby) Cundall, ?, Ella Frape
Source: Ella Frape

Part III
Life In Boroughbridge

Chapter 19
Evacuees

At the time of the Blitz in London and other cities, anyone who had spare rooms in Boroughbridge was pressed to take in evacuees. The Boroughbridge area took in many throughout the course of the war. Service personnel and those involved with war work in the local area were also housed by local families.

Bank manager George Smailes's wife Mary Smailes was the local Billeting Officer, responsible for allocating accommodation for evacuees (see also her daughters' recollections, p168).

Mary Smailes

Maureen Douglas

Maureen Douglas stayed in Boroughbridge for about eight months during 1941 before returning to her parents' home in the North East. The following are Maureen's written memories.

"In the spring of 1941 at the age of twelve years I came to Boroughbridge as an evacuee from Tyneside, accompanied by my five-year-old brother Patrick.

We were to stay with our elderly grandparents, Mr and Mrs Coates, who lived in the High Street, where I had stayed on holiday many times before, so Boroughbridge was well known to me. I was not fearful in the slightest.

We attended the Primary School on York Road, where we received a good education, and made friends very easily, one of whom I am still in touch with.

Coming here was a delight for me because of the freedom to roam in the wonderful countryside, far away from the air raids of the North-East. In fact one wasn't aware of the war at all, apart from the soldiers billeted around about. Rationing didn't seem to be a problem; there was always plenty of good plain home-cooked food. Occasionally we had fish and chips as a treat, bought from the fish shop in High Street.

On certain Sundays we were treated to the sight of the soldiers marching to the church, to the sound of their band playing exhilarating music, which the children loved.

Grandma had a couple of soldiers' wives staying with her. She had a big house and filled it, so the husbands visited frequently. We still have photographs of those happy occasions.

Two uncles came on leave from the army and spoilt us children with attention they gave us. I treasure those memories as some of the happiest of my life, and I'm now fortunate to reside permanently here in Boroughbridge my favourite place.

On domestic life in Boroughbridge in the war years, I should mention that Boroughbridge had little or no sanitation in 1941 [*ed: actually, mostly there was fine sanitation in Boroughbridge at that time!—but evidently this was Maureen's experience*]. We used day toilets 'up the yard', emptied by the 'night soil' men now and then. There was no running water or taps in the house, all water was carried from the Fountain in white enamel buckets kept solely for the purpose. Bathing was in a tin bath by the fire, once a week whether we needed it or not. A good wash daily before bed was the norm.

We did however have a gas supply, but not electricity, so light was supplied by a central gas light in the ceiling, or oil lamp or candles. By the standards of the day Grandma was modern, because she had a gas cooker, but she still used the side oven heated from the fire in the lounge.

I learned to knit during my time here, and well remember the sense of pride and achievement when I completed a pair of grey socks on four needles, and turning the heels all by myself. I wore my green gloves with embroidered backs with pride, all my own work."

Barbara (Seaman) Breckon's memories

Barbara and Walter Seaman

My father Walter Seaman was employed as civilian engineer at Dishforth throughout the war. We lived in New Row, Boroughbridge, opposite the Police Station.

Mum took in many evacuees and lodgers during the war. They were from Liverpool, Newcastle and London. I remember two boys from London and a girl called Daphne who caused Mum and Dad a lot of worry, always getting into trouble. They all brought nits with them, but only the clothes they stood up in.

Jim and Norma Sprung were evacuees from Liverpool who lodged with the us, and also, I think, with Taylors next door to Ramsdales, butchers in St James' Square. We kept up our friendship after the war.

Bank manager George Smailes's wife Mary was the local person responsible for allocating evacuees. I think George and Annie Dean also had some involvement. They lived adjoining the fish shop at the bottom of Valuation Lane.

(See more of Barbara Breckon's memories, p166).

Mike Tasker's memories

Next door to us in New Row, a Mr Price lived on his own. He had evacuees from London staying with him for a short time in the early stages of the war. There was a boy about my age Paul Charman, with his mother, there may have been an elder sister too. They were not very friendly, and returned to London when the worst of the bombing had subsided. Their stay next to us in Boroughbridge was relatively brief.

Mrs Seaman, two doors up New Row from us, had evacuees from Newcastle despite having two children of her own, Barbara and Peter. I can't remember the names of the evacuees, but there was a lad about my age I started to play with. He was a nice friendly lad and I was getting on with him famously, but I very quickly picked up a Geordie accent from him which my mother thought was dreadful, so unfortunately the friendship was not encouraged. They too were not long before they returned home.

Later in the war during the time of the doodlebugs and V2s, there were further evacuees, Mrs Godley, her son Ron who was quite a talented artist, and her nephew Kenneth Lack. Their house in London had been bombed out, so they had nowhere to live. They stayed until almost the end of the war. Kenneth was about my age, I made good friends with him. We wrote to each other very briefly after the war, he sent me a post card from his holiday in Herne Bay, but to my regret the correspondence did not last and we lost touch.

Picture by Ron Godley in Dorothy Tasker's Autograph Book

(See more of Mike Tasker's memories, p161.)

Geoff Craggs' memories

As soon as war was declared, Boroughbridge had a good number of evacuees sent from Leeds to live with local families; Leeds was regarded as a target for German bombers. I remember we had two boys come to stay with us at Stump Cross; they had no socks, had plimsolls, ragged jumpers and NITS! They shared their nits with all of us at Boroughbridge Primary School, which was generous. That was my first encounter with a fine tooth comb, and perhaps theirs with a bath and hair wash. I remember the Leeds evacuees went home after only a few weeks, but by then other evacuees came in from as far as London.

(See more of Geoff Craggs' memories, p157.)

Cyril Gudgeon's memories

Cyril remembers an incident in 1940 involving an evacuee lad, name forgotten, who stayed at Mrs Leaning's shop on Main street.

Along with Bobby Renton, he was helping with a lorry transporting sugar beet from Aldborough to the Sugar Beet factory in York. It was driven by Frank Tillet from Grafton. At the unloading area in the factory, Bobby Renton was climbing up the back of the lorry which was being backed up to a wall. Tragically, he was crushed against the wall and killed. The evacuee lad had to dash to the front of the lorry shouting for the driver to stop. Cyril was a pall bearer at Bobby's funeral. He was 14 years old.

Source: interview with the author

Florence Capstick's memories

New Row. Had several evacuees, particularly remembered was Jean Burns from Leeds who kept up the contact well after the war. Also evacuees from London.

Source: Michael Wilson

Chapter 20
Domestic Life

The war was a time of worry, with menfolk away in the war, soldiers and airmen everywhere, shortages of many things, and an atmosphere of danger ever close. In these times people were thrown together in a spirit of survival, which produced a uniquely strong community spirit and neighbourliness.

Shopping

Wartime shopping was of course a world away from the shopping of today. Shopping was from 9.00am to 5.30pm, with no shopping on Sundays. The High Street was very busy with many small shops, all with their own speciality. Shopping was an every day job, and very time consuming it was too, despite the fact that there was very little choice compared with the dazzling array on offer today, and even then, the basic commodities were rationed. You had to remember to take your ration card. Queues were commonplace.

There was no self service, the goods were on shelves behind the sales counter, and each customer was dealt with in turn. Nothing was pre-packed, no plastic bags. Each item had to be taken from the shelves by the shop assistant, weighed out, bagged or wrapped in grease-proof paper as necessary, and handed over to the customer to be placed in her shopping basket. If for example you wanted butter or cheese from the grocery shop, it would be individually cut and weighed out to the amount you wanted, or to the ration you were allowed. A family order could take perhaps half an hour, with customers behind waiting their turn. The shop assistant would write down the price of each item, then add up the total cost—no electric tills, no room for shop assistants who couldn't add up the pounds, shillings and pence.

Shortages were common and queues were the norm. You had to keep your ear to the ground to get to know when special things arrived on the shelves, or you'd miss them.

There was no such thing as whipping round the supermarket and getting a week's shopping. Besides, nobody had fridges or freezers, so perishable things would not keep. A cool pantry was all that was available to most households. And cars were a rarity, so you had to carry everything you bought, generally not very much.

Shops

From the Black Bull down the left hand side were

- Martin's Shoe shop
- Linfoot's Saddler and Leather shop
- Hair Dressers
- Bacon's Agricultural Produce
- Hettie Ellis's Vegetable shop
- Pybus's Newspaper shop
- Burley's Butcher shop
- Scaife's Haberdashery shop
- Moss's Grocery shop
- Mrs Bryant, Sweet shop
- Billy Coates, Cobblers
- Richardson's Telephone Exchange
- Wilson's Antique and Furniture shop
- Black Lion

On the right had side were

- Ernest Robinson's Grocery shop
- Tasker's (later Waddington's) Paint shop
- Wombwell's Fish & Chip shop
- Walton's Vegetable shop
- Preston's Clothing and Workwear shop
- Tyreman-Sturdy Chemist's shop
- Thompson's Coal Merchant

On Fishergate were

- Chibby Binns's Bakery
- Morten's Bakery
- Hubert Pullen's Barbershop
- Mrs Davey's Sweet shop
- Johnny Pickering's Leather Shop
- Palmer's Grocery shop
- Hewson's Haberdashery, Clothing Shop
- Charlie Potter's Hardware shop

Along the top of St James's Square were

- Whitaker's Bakery,
- Ramsdale's Butchers
- Hope's Paint shop
- Mrs Ellis's Sweet and Biscuit shop
- Windmill Cafe (taken over by the army)
- Benson's Sweet shop
- Farrer's, Mitch Mudd's Plant & Vegetable shop

On the opposite side of the square was

- Carass's Butcher shop
- Basil Johnston's Auctioneers

Fish and Chips

Wombwell's fish and chip shop, half-way down High Street, was one of the most thriving shops in the town. Very popular with the soldiers from the army camp, there were often queues stretching half way down the street, who would take their fish and chips wrapped in newspaper.

Other shops

All watches were mechanical in the era before digital, and if they packed up, as they often did, they would need repair. "Clocky" Wise was a local repair specialist, he lived in a cottage on York Road—one of the real characters of Boroughbridge at the time. He may have been good at watch repairs, but if you went to pick up your watch hoping that he had repaired it, you would discover that he had hundreds of watches all in repair, and finding yours was like looking for a needle in a haystack. Sometimes he would ask you to come back the next day to give him a chance to find it. A really nice man, but organisation and procedure were not part of his make-up.

Charlie Potter's Hardware shop was also an interesting purchasing adventure. Charlie was also a very nice and helpful guy, he looked like Mr Pickwick with his moustache, grey hair and hat. In his window he had two round rotating turntables on which his wares were displayed. There were nails, screws, tools of all description on these turntables, some rusty, I don't think they were ever dusted. But whatever you wanted Charlie would have it somewhere, perhaps in a store room at the back of the shop. Not good to be in a hurry if you went there, but if you had the time you usually got what you wanted.

Mrs Pratt had a sweet and cigarette shop in New Row, popular with school kids for sweets, but in times of rationing there was not much available. Two ounces of sweets a week (one Kit Kat bar) did not go very far.

Milk Deliveries

Most of the town got their milk from Sadler's farm. Mary Dodsworth used to visit each house with a churn of milk, and would ladle out the required amount into the householder's jug, fresh from the cow each day. She had a special ladle for cream, we used to get two gills [two quarter-pint measures] periodically.

Gardening

Everyone grew their own vegetables if they could, flowers were a luxury. Many had hens in the garden as a source of eggs, then meat when the hens were no longer laying. Chicken was an absolute luxury.

Washing and Cleaning

Another time-consuming job in the days before washing machines and vacuum cleaners.

Clothes would typically be washed once a week, using a coal fired boiler. Peggy tubs were widely used for washing things that could not be boiled and for rinsing things out. A peggy or posser would be used to bash the clothes about in the peggy tub to get them clean. Then the clothes would be put through a wringing machine to squeeze out the excess water, and hung up to dry on a washing line in the garden. Clothes props were in regular use to prop up long lines. In winter there would be a clothes rack, perhaps in the kitchen, to dry the clothes. In the days before synthetic fibres all the clothes would need ironing, and for large families this could be an all day job.

In many households it would be unusual to have fitted carpets. There would be a square or oblong carpet in the middle of the room with lino round the edges. Vacuum cleaners were not common, a hand push Ewbank type sweeper would commonly be used to keep the carpet clean, but once a year in the summer, carpets would be taken up, hung outside on a line and beaten with a cane carpet beater to bash out the dust.

The steps outside front and back doors would be washed regularly and scoured with a creamy-yellow scouring stone. ie a border on the outside of the step. This is something which simply does not happen these days, but was a regular feature in Boroughbridge at that time. Had to keep up appearances!

Refuse Collection

Dustbins were emptied on a regular basis, I think once a week, but the refuse consisted mainly of ash from the coal fires, with some glass, broken pots and tins.

Newspapers were burnt to start the fires, so they were rarely rubbish. There would be very little waste food, wasting food was almost regarded as a crime in times of such shortage. Anything that would burn was thrown into the fire.

Coal and Gas

Domestic coal fires were practically universal for housing during the war years, the heat from a fire back boiler would provide hot water and heat for the room. Everyone had to have a coal house shed or bunker. George Wright would deliver the coal, he would carry 1cwt [one hundred-weight, about 50kg] sacks on his back from his wagon to each house. He would of course be covered in coal dust. Coal was on allocation, 4 bags per month.

Boroughbridge had its own gas works, owned by Lofthouses, producing coal gas, on the side of the Great North Road, next to the river Tutt. Street lighting was by gas lights, and most households had a gas cooker. When lighting was allowed after the blackout, Charlie Reynard used to go round each street lamp to light it up, then turn it off at day break.

A by-product from the coal gas production at the gasworks was coke. It was not rationed, and was sold on to the general public. It served as a useful supplement for the domestic coal fires. In some ways it was better than coal. It was off ration, cheaper, cleaner and lasted well on the fire giving a nice red glow. It was however difficult to get burning, so the fire had to be started off with coal. The coke gave very little flame.

Transport

Buses and Trains

West Yorkshire Road Car buses ran hourly between Boroughbridge and Harrogate, and the United Bus Company ran services between York and Ripon via Boroughbridge, every 2 hours.

A striking feature about the West Yorkshire buses was that they were sometimes powered by gas, the gas tank in a trailer pulled behind the buses or alternatively on the roof of the bus.

The trains were the alternative means of transport from Boroughbridge to Knaresborough and Harrogate, but the train station was more remote from the centre of town.

The trains were used extensively for goods transport.

Cars

There were very few cars on the roads, some had been requisitioned for war work, others were unable to get petrol. Most of the vehicles on the roads were military traffic.

Garages

Reed's Garage was the main repair garage, I suspect the military kept them going, and the filling station outside Kelly's Cafe was the busiest petrol station, handily situated on the Great North Road.

Other garages were the Canal Garage, Nicholson and Slater, Fairbanks, and Clapham's.

School

For junior school, everyone walked to school, that was normal. At the start of the war, some junior classes were held in the Parochial Hall, alongside St James's church, but by September 1941 both Juniors and Seniors were accommodated in the new York Road school. Periodically the Parochial Hall would be used for overspill as evacuees came and went. The class rooms were spartan in comparison with today's schools, with no pictures on the wall, just a big blackboard on the wall at the front of the class. In the days before biros the desks all had inkwells, and each class had a designated inkwell monitor from the pupils, whose job it was to keep the inkwells filled. Blotting paper was issued to everyone, and in regular use. Blots on the work books were not well regarded. Milk was also available to all pupils for a small payment, so there was also a milk monitor.

Cod liver oil was available once a week, there was a bowl at the end of the corridor, everyone had to bring their own spoon, queue up in the corridor and take one spoonful. The facial expressions as the pupils downed their spoonful were a sight to behold, but we were told it was good for us and would keep us healthy.

Caning was a regular punishment for misbehaviour, always administered by headmaster Gaffa Frape.

Playtime in the school yard usually took the form of football with a tennis ball for the boys, whilst the girls played hopscotch and other games.

The toilets were part of the building but were outside.

Religious Services

Services in both church and chapel were well attended, and there were regular army and airforce parades from the camps, up Church Lane to St James's Church for Sunday morning service.

Ronald Kettlewell was the vicar of St James's at the beginning of the war, followed by Mervyn Evers in 1944.

Pubs

The Black Bull, Malt Shovel, Black Lion, Three Horse Shoes and Three Greyhounds were the main pubs in the town, with the Grantham Arms and the Anchor Inn just over the river.

In Aldborough were the Ship Inn and Penrose's Aldeburg Arms, in Roecliffe the Crown, in Langthorpe the Fox and Hounds.

The Black Bull and the Malt Shovel were particularly popular with the Forces.

Telephone Exchange

There was a telephone exchange down High Street next door to Bobby Wilson's shop.

Candle Maker

Throughout the war Mr Chipchase had a workshop down Back Lane for making candles. The smells from his workshop were really something else, but in the event of power being cut (which did not happen often in Boroughbridge) there would certainly have been a big demand for his wares.

Cattle Market

Tuesday was Auction Day at the cattle market—a regular event throughout the war. Sheep and cattle were brought in from local farms to be sold, and for farmers to get together for their regular local gossip. Basil Johnson's auctioneering technique was a spectacle in itself, his machine gun speed of speech was unequalled anywhere. He certainly got the business done in double quick time.

Sadler's Farm

From today's perspective it seems hardly believable that there was a farm right in the middle of the town. You could access Sadler's farm directly from High Street, next to Tyreman Sturdy's Chemists Shop (later George Moore's), but for regular farm use, the access was on to Back Lane, alongside the army camp. Billy Sadler used to run the farm on behalf of his Aunt, Miss Harriot Sadler, the owner. He had a herd of cows which were brought to the farm daily from their field now Ladywell Road, for milking. They were brought in up and down and Back Lane (then known as "Cow Clap Lane") and Church Lane. What a mess it was too. In the absence of traffic Church Lane was used as a playground for the local children—their cricket games were often played on a very sticky wicket after the cows had been up and down.

Chapter 21
Entertainment and Social Activities

Dances

With so many young men in the forces in Boroughbridge, in the Army camps and also from the RAF at Dishforth, the dances in the area were very popular, particularly at the Crown Hotel, which had a lovely sprung dance floor. Many a romance with local girls began at these dances, and ended up in marriage.

Dances were often organised by the Army or RAF from Dishforth with their own military bands. Sid Pullan's band also played at Boroughbridge dances and other dance halls all around the area. Known members of his band were Arthur (fiddler) Buck, playing the violin and Norman Salter playing the Double Bass, and Sid playing the piano. (The only recorded music at that time was on bakelite discs: the era of disco music was still some years away.)

Many local girls met up with soldiers and airmen at these dances and several married soldiers from the camp. Among them were Julie Reed who married Cliff Calley, Pat Smith who married Alf Stokes, Winnie Steele who married Frank Wilson, and Lilly Binns who married Billy Weaver. There were several others. Since all the local young men were away in the forces anyway, it could be regarded as a natural course of events.

Pictures

In an age before television, the cinema was of course a very popular form of entertainment, particularly with youngsters.

At the Methodist Chapel in Horsefair, periodically Ronald Howgate used to run black and white films. He had a collection of movie pictures from before the war, the entrance fee was one penny, so they were called the "Penny Pictures".

Breakdowns were frequent with the old celluloid films, each breakdown followed by howls and groans from the viewers - these were an entertainment in themselves! There would be an interval of black-out and chatter, whilst the projectionist pieced together the breaks in the film, then started projection up again. It was after all the age of "make do and mend".

The films on show featured Mother Riley (Where's mi daughter Kitty?), Abbott and Costello, George Formby and others, mostly comedy films.

Films were also shown periodically by the army in the Crown Hotel. Dave Watson remembers viewing them back to front from outside—that way he didn't have to pay!

Swimming

On a warm summer evening, swimming in the river was a regular activity in the area around the Salmon Ladders. The good swimmers would dive and swim in the top "sam" and also upstream from the weir. The star performers would show their diving prowess by diving from the railway bridge, it was a long way down, and certainly not for the faint hearted. The beginners would learn swimming in the bottom "sam" which was only two feet deep, and then work up the salmon ladders as they became more proficient.

Over the bottom of the bottom "sam" is a ledge about a foot wide, but one step out and it runs into deep water, which I found out to my cost. As a six year old I was in the bottom "sam" as a beginner paddling about, when I ventured over the edge on to the ledge to explore, stepped out a bit further and found myself straight into the deep water. I remember hitting the bottom three times, coming to the surface gasping for breath, I was certainly close to drowning. Then I felt arms around me, Willy Horner had come to the rescue, he pulled me back to dry land. I owe my life to him.

Cubs and Scouts

The cubs were run by Mrs Morris (Baaloo) from Springfield Road, they met in the hayloft attached to the vicarage on Church Lane. We learned the "dib dib dob", etc.

The scouts were run by Mrs Spencer and Mr Akers, they also met in the hayloft.

Brownies and guides were also active.

Parochial Hall

This was a meeting place for whist drives, dominoes, occasional amateur musical concerts and other social events. Occasionally there would be film shows here, and very occasionally also dances. Every so often Mrs Violet Topham would organise entertainment for the local children, singing and fancy dress events which some of the soldiers also visited, perhaps as a reminder of their own children.

Church Choir

This was popular with young lads who could sing. Chibby Binns was the organist and Charlie Green used to be the organ pumper (there was no electric organ until just after the war).

Mr Robinson, Mr Ellis and Mr Jeff sang the men's part, Mrs Buck and Mary Burley sang soprano.

Radio and Music

In the days before universal television, the radio was of course the media for news and entertainment. The radio would often be powered by the heavy lead acid accumulators which had to be re-charged periodically—not at all user friendly. The news of the declaration of war against Germany would be heard by most people over the radio.

Entertainment programs would be music, comedian programs, Arthur Askey, Kenneth Horne etc, quiz programs (Wilfred Pickles) and other light entertainment programs—along with a good dose of war-time propaganda.

We had a wind-up gramophone with bakelite records for music. It was quite good until it ran out of power, when it gradually played slower and slower until the music disappeared altogether, a sound imprinted on my mind which I shall never forget. Later versions were electrically powered—much better than having to wind them up.

Newspapers

The National newspapers were much more widely read than these days as a source of visual information, with photographs and other details not part of the radio broadcasts. The local newspaper was the Knaresborough Post and Boroughbridge Herald.

Dandy and Beano were very popular childrens' comics. My favourite was Desperate Dan in the Dandy.

Public Houses

George Wager, landlord of the Malt Shovel

These were of course very popular with the troops in the town and the airmen from Dishforth. The Black Bull was a favourite haunt of the Canadian airmen from Dishforth, whilst the Malt Shovel, being so close to the army camp, was favoured by the troops.

Other favoured pubs were the Black Lion and the Three Horse Shoes.

Chapter 22
The Bridge Collapse of 1945

On the date of the General Election, July 5th 1945, the bridge carrying the Great North Road (the old A1) over the river Ure collapsed under the 180 ton combined weight of three Pickfords lorries, one towing and two pushing, and a bogey carrying an 80 ton steel casting from Sheffield to Falkirk. Surprisingly perhaps, it was the southbound lane (the eastern, downstream side of the bridge) that collapsed and fell into the river: the rest of the bridge still stood, though clearly unusable for vehicles. The surprise isn't hard to explain when you look at the bend in the road before the bridge, and consider the huge size and articulation of the vehicle train carrying the casting.

The collapsed east side of the bridge, lorry and casting below, spectators above.
From the Yorkshire Post and Leeds Mercury, Friday 6th July 1945

The whole town went down to see this spectacular sight, and it was widely reported, with photographs in the Knaresborough Post and Boroughbridge Herald and other newspapers.

The news of the bridge is well known and recorded, not so well known is that it took a major operation to get the casting out of the river. The lorries were recovered relatively quickly, but the casting was a different matter. The recovery team had to build a massive ramp from Mill Lane down to the casting in the river. The casting was being moved at not more than 2 feet per hour. It took 17 days to get it out on to a huge bogey, and away. It took nearly four years to rebuild the bridge.

Chapter 22. The Bridge Collapse of 1945

Under the bridge   **Over the bridge**

What happened to the Great North Road traffic in the meantime? Well, as luck would have it Boroughbridge was able to live up to its name, it borrowed a bridge! The Royal Engineers had built a Bailey bridge over the river Ure, designed to take light army traffic, one way only. So there it was, when the Great North Road bridge collapsed, merely under heavy load. I doubt whether the town of Boroughbridge has ever known such luck. For the next few months, the traffic was routed through the army camp and over the girder bridge, on an alternating one way traffic system. Of course the traffic just after the war was minimal compared with today's traffic on the A1, but still enough to cause enormous dislocation.

After some months a more substantial two-way girder bridge was erected by Dorman Long on the upstream side of the damaged old stone bridge, and traffic transferred to that. It was some time before the Army actually removed the one-track bridge. Repairs on the original bridge were only completed some three and a half years after the collapse.

Chapter 22. The Bridge Collapse of 1945

Aerial view
Taken in March 1946, this shows the collapsed bridge, the Dorman Long temporary bridge, and the even more temporary Bailey bridge. The route through the Army camp can be seen, and the disruption to traffic easily imagined.
Photo: English Heritage archives. Used with permission.

Chapter 22. The Bridge Collapse of 1945

Chapter 23
Personal Memories

Geoff Craggs

Geoff Craggs served seven terms as mayor of Boroughbridge. Below is his story as given to the Boroughbridge Historical Society some years ago.

Geoff Craggs, 2000   Godfrey Craggs, 1939

Outbreak of war

I was 7 years old when war broke out in 1939, and I vividly remember exactly what I was doing when my Dad came and told me. He had heard the news on the wireless (not called "radio" then!), and came out into the garden where I was sitting on my Triang pedal car, which I had outgrown but would not part with, to say that war had broken out and he would be going to fight the Germans.

My Dad had been in the Territorial Army in the early 30s, but was invalided out with rheumatic fever apparently. This did not stop him being passed "A1" in 1939. He was in fact 34 years old, and because he worked for West Riding County Council as a gang foreman on road building, he could have been exempted from military service. However, the Royal Engineers needed skilled road men, and recruited round all County Councils. My Dad volunteered along with many other WRCC employees, went to Pontefract Barracks for enlistment, and they all went out as part of the British Expeditionary Force to France as 116th Road Construction Company in late 1939.

Evacuees and school

As soon as war was declared, Boroughbridge had a good number of evacuees sent from Leeds to live with local families. Leeds was regarded as a target for German bombers. I remember we had two boys come to stay with us at Stump Cross. They had no socks, plimsolls, ragged jumpers and ... NITS! They shared the nits with all of us at Boroughbridge Primary School, which was generous. That was my first encounter with a fine tooth comb, and I think theirs with a bath and hair wash.

Because the school was now overcrowded, (and in those days the present Primary School housed both Primary and Secondary Modern children), Class 2 (Miss Brown's class) and I think Miss Byers' Class 3, moved to the old school up Church Lane (more or less on the site of the Health Centre), and had a great time, away from the rest of the school. (In passing, it is one of Boroughbridge's great "what ifs" that the then parish Council in the late 60s did not buy this building, which was used for a great number of local activities – including the library.) The only drawback was that we had to go out to the rudimentary toilets! I remember the Leeds evacuees were home after only a few weeks, but by then other evacuees came in from as far away as London, but we could move back to the "new" school.

At home

My Dad had gone to France by then, and we had letters from him, but I was at home with my stepmother; I remember she had to go out to work, at Miss Mudd's Dairy, Aldborough, where she had worked before marrying Dad (my own Mother had died in 1935), and she had to work very hard, delivering milk with Tom Archer. We also had to take lodgers, as a lot of civilian engineers had come to work at RAF Dishforth, and of course the Army had come to Boroughbridge. The first lodgers we had were a Mr and Mrs Ingram, from Coventry. He was an engineer for Armstrong Whitworth, and worked on the engines of the Whitley bombers at Dishforth. I remember he had a Riley 9 car, which impressed me, as we had never had a car! Whilst they were with us, their house in Coventry was destroyed in the blitz, and they went back to Coventry (this must have been around 1942/3).

I mentioned we had lodgers; after the Ingrams we had Mr and Mrs Jones, he was another civilian worker at Dishforth.

Bike and pumps

Mrs Jones was very good at giving me first aid after my many mishaps with my bike – most memorable being after oiling the chain, turning the chain wheel round at great speed with my index finger, and trapping said digit between chain and sprocket. I still have the scar.

What else did we do as wartime kids? Roamed the fields around, followed the soldiers, hoping to pick up bullet cases (we did, from time to time). Went to the various fund raising events, like "Wings for Victory". One of the most memorable of these was the sterling performance by the local volunteer firemen one day, when they staged a "rescue" from the top window of what is now Greenwood and Company's building. They had a very long ladder, one of them went up it to "rescue" a damsel in distress (a dummy), and had a terrible time coming back down – chiefly because his "colleagues" were pumping water at him from an old manual pump. This machine lived in Joe Clark's yard in St Helena, and was loaned to the York Castle Museum for safe keeping when the volunteer fire service moved from the rear of Greenwood's butchers. I have tried unsuccessfully to get it back for Boroughbridge, but sadly the York people deny they ever had it.

Precautions

People often ask "were there air raid shelters". There were two in the school grounds, on the grass between the school and the Aldborough/York Road junction, one was for the juniors and one for the seniors. I remember we had to go into the shelter when the siren went (this was on the Police Station, and went off for tests fairly regularly); we had to wear our gas masks, which tasted and smelt of rubber, and which we had to carry everywhere in a cardboard box with string to go round your neck. It was damp, dark and cold down the shelter, and I remember we once had to sit with tear gas in the shelter to see if the masks worked. They did (sort of).

Chapter 23. Personal Memories   Geoff Craggs

Rationing

The biggest problem for kids was sweets. We had been used to having a reasonable amount of toffees, chocolate before the war (governed by your pocket money and how indulgent your parents and grandparents were): suddenly that all stopped, and the ration amounted to about a bar of chocolate a week (I think). Additionally, whilst you could get apples, pears and plums during the season (either legally or by scrumping), after that — - nothing. Once a week there was a small delivery of bananas or oranges to Miss Ellis's shop in High Street, and if you queued and were lucky you might find yourself with one banana or one orange. However, necessity being the mother of invention, there were alternatives.

In 1942 I sat and passed the County Minor scholarship to King James Grammar School in Knaresborough, and a whole new world opened up in the form of Mr Lawrance's Oldest Chymist Shop (it WAS spelt like that) and his rich source of liquorice root (advisable to be chewed and swallowed only in small quantities, for obvious reasons) and cinnamon sticks. This diet supplemented by Clarkson's halfpenny teacakes and — wonder of wonders — half a single block of Lyon's ice cream (some of you will remember that these were small cylinders about 2 inches in height and the same in diameter) from Mrs Woodward's shop opposite the bus station. This happened only very rarely, and usually when you were "skint".

As far as meat, eggs and other groceries were concerned, I cannot remember a shortage, living in the country; the limit was as to whether we could afford them! I remember that Miss Mudd kept pigs, as she was rightly famous for her ham and egg teas, which were popular with the aircrew from Linton and Dishforth; one pig was called Hitler, and became such a pet that Miss Mudd could not bear to see it killed, commerce prevailed however, and Hitler became bacon, pork and ham.

Military presence

To "us kids", all that was happening around us was a big adventure; Army regiments coming and going – looking back over almost 70 years, it is hard to remember what regiments actually came to the town; I have checked with those contemporaries who were around at the time, and we all have the same problem! I know we had Scottish, Yorkshire regiments, the Pioneer Corps and Royal Engineers, but how many and when ... it's all gone. I know that officers were living in Boroughbridge Hall, Aldborough Hall, "other ranks" were in Bacon's shop (now Peter Greenwood's building), and in Nissen huts where the houses are on Aldborough Road, between there and the Hall, and in the fields on York Road which became Springfield Drive.

As a child, it was all very exciting, with soldiers and airmen everywhere, some ATS girls, Army and RAF lorries whizzing around (we even had 60 foot long lorries carrying bits of aeroplanes about, parked up in Fishergate and on Horsefair, to marvel at). Planes flying about, night and day – mainly Whitley and Wellington bombers, but a few Spitfires, and one Sunday (possibly in 1940) I was biking to Stump Cross from my Granny's on Aldborough Road when I definitely saw a Messerschmitt go over, followed by a Spitfire ... HONESTLY!

Tragedy

In 1940 my life was changed. Dad had come home for Christmas 1939, and gave me an Army knife, which I still have; he went back to France after 7 days leave, and Mum and I never saw him again. In June 1940, after the Dunkirk evacuation, he, the rest of his Company and up to 9,000 other British, French and Canadian personnel, plus nurses and French civilians were on the "Lancastria" when she was bombed and sank with the loss of thousands of lives, including my Father. For the rest of the War he was officially "missing, presumed killed", with a pittance by way of pension to my Mum. The whole "Lancastria" business is still a closed file. For an 8-year-old boy, devastation; the fact that Dad was "missing" was the great hope that kept Mum and me going: he might turn up as a prisoner. Of course, this didn't happen. After a couple of years, hope went, but we had learnt to live with it and coped. Looking back, people were kind and supportive to us, and life as a small boy still went on.

Ranging wide

Coal was rationed and I used to have a "bogey" which I made with the help of my Grandad. I used to take it to the Gas House on a Saturday morning for a sack of (unrationed) coke, which I hauled back to Stump Cross to keep the fire going. Although we lived in a new house, it still had only a fire range for cooking, though we did have a small gas ring for boiling the kettle. My bike and my "Bogey" were my real treasures; I'd bike all over, mainly with my best pal Bill Rennison, as far afield as Studley Deer Park and Fountains — this when we were 10 years old, and no-one had any concerns about this — dark days for the nations, but still golden days for children.

Another adventure, incredible to think of now, was that on what is now the A168 but what was then the A1, which went through Boroughbridge, south through Stump Cross, up Gibbet Hill and Ornhams, we used to choose our times between the infrequent lorries, and hurtle down Gibbet Hill, past Stump Cross, Kelly's Café and nearly to the "Rec"! In winter, before the gritting lorries came round, you could do the same thing on a sledge (also down Aldborough Hill, though you had to sneak past Grandad's house on Hill Top! Don't try it now.

Bombers

York was heavily bombed, and some relations came to stay with my grandparents when their home was damaged in York. I can remember them as not being very nice people, and my grandparents being glad to see them go home. On many nights I can remember the sirens went, and we sat downstairs under the stairs and listened to the German planes going over, and hearing the bombs falling on York.

In 1944, a Lancaster bomber crashed on Howe Hill at Aldborough, two fields from where my grandparents lived, and going across to see the site, tragically all the crew were killed, but the Aldborough policeman Jim Harley, who was a friend of ours, was decorated for trying to save them.

Bands

What was there to do? Many lads joined the Air Scouts, and we met in a loft at the vicarage. The Scouts were run by a Mr Akers and Mrs Spencer (the wife of the Head of the Secondary School). We had a great time learning knots and doing all the other things Scouts do.

I think it was called Air Scouts because of clothes rationing, we only needed our school flannels, grey shirts, and a blue beret, plus the neckerchief, as opposed to the harder-to-obtain regular Scout uniform. Good fun, until Mr and Mrs Spencer moved on.

There was also the British Legion Silver Band, which some of us joined towards the end of the war; this was led by Mr Ingledew (Pauline Phillip's grandfather), and we practiced above what is now the Social Club. Bernard Harcourt, who had been bandmaster of one of the regiments in Boroughbridge, married Joan Davey, and he took over the band, which grew from strength to strength until – sadly – it disbanded in 1955.

One abiding memory is of the Nissen huts off York Road being occupied by squatters at the end of the war, by returning servicemen and their families who were homeless, and of "sailing" between the huts in a tin bath when the snow melted (Springfield did not get that name for nothing!) – again with Bill Rennison and others.

More? Much more, but that's enough for now.

Mike Tasker

1945   2012

Early memories

There was no escape for Boroughbridge from military involvement in WW2. Its central location on the A1 road made it an ideal location for an army staging post. A camp was established in Boroughbridge Hall and grounds, with the Crown Hotel, Three Greyhounds, Three Horse Shoes, Windmill Cafe, Hotel Cottages and the Malt Shovel Inn also used by the army. Later there were army Nissen huts between Springfield Road and York Road. There was constant activity and movement by soldiers, and with Dishforth Aerodrome just two miles away, Linton, Topcliffe and other airfields also close, aerial activity was ever present over the town throughout the war. This was the backdrop for my childhood in Boroughbridge in WW2.

Even as a three year old when war broke out, perhaps surprisingly I do have some still clear memories of those early years of the war. My earliest military memory pre-dates the war – the artillery field gun from the first world war in Hall Square, just the thing young children love to clamber about on. I had lots of fun playing on it, but sadly, along with railings and other non-essential metal objects, the gun disappeared in the early years of the war, no doubt to be melted down to be re-cycled into much needed war materials

ARP

Dad was the deputy head of the Air Raid Precautions (ARP) organisation for the Boroughbridge area from before the start of the war, and as such, was involved in the distribution of gas masks once the war had started. I remember at one time our lounge being filled from floor to ceiling with gas masks, all in their cardboard boxes. Gas masks for all-comers, some for new babies in which the baby could be totally enclosed, red Mickey Mouse ones for toddlers and infants, and others for older children and adults. They were quickly distributed to the populace of the town, and soon we were able to return our lounge to normal living space. There was a camp bed in our dining room, where ARP wardens stayed the night on duty. We had a black stand-up bakelite telephone, which my father had for his painting and decorating business, and I imagine that was used for the ARP purposes also. Our phone number was Boroughbridge 147 – phones were of course relatively few back then. My father also had a car, loaned from his brother, my uncle Harry, who was abroad working in Sudan. It was a 1933 maroon Austin 10, registration JJ355. Dad used it for his business, and I imagine it was also used on ARP business. It seems that ARP business was often conducted in pubs in the local villages, and coming back from such a meeting in the Crown at Roecliffe, Dad's car met disaster. There was serious flooding from the river Ure, probably in the winter of 1941, and dad's car was caught in the floods in a dip under the railway bridge on the road home. He had to abandon the car and walk home. I remember going with him next day to see his car in the water, you could just see the roof, a total disaster. When the floods receded the car was towed back home, but it spent the rest of the war up on chocks in our garage. I don't know how dad managed to continue his ARP role without a car, perhaps he resorted to cycling.

Amongst the papers left by my father when he died I found the ARP log book for the early years of the war. The records confirm the frequent presence of enemy aircraft in the area. In particular, a red alert entry for 25th April 1941 records hearing the dropping of "two sticks of bombs. All windows and doors shook." This corresponds exactly to the bombing of Linton Airfield, some 7 miles away, clearly heard in Boroughbridge. Remarkably too, the blast cracked a pane of glass in our landing window.

ARP wardens recorded in the log book were Herbert Tasker, (Deputy Head Warden), Arthur Buck (Blacksmith), Arthur Linfoot (Sadler), Sid Pullen (Plantsman), Maurice Calvert (Teacher), E Burley (Butcher), Paul Armstrong, Ronnie Topham (Post Office & Shop Keeper), F J Hind, Rev R M Kettlewell (Vicar), E B Paul, H Paul, S Armstrong, Geo W Mudd, Paul Pullan, Special Constables Watson S/C462, Hope S/C451, Morten S/C, Nicholson S/C, W Waddington, and PC Blacklock.

Evacuees

At the time of the Blitz in London and other cities, anyone who had spare rooms in Boroughbridge was pressed to take in evacuees. Next door to us in New Row, a Mr Price lived on his own. He had evacuees from London staying with him for a short time. There was a boy about my age Paul Charman, with his mother, there may have been an elder sister too. They were not very friendly, and returned to London when the worst of the bombing had subsided. Their stay in Boroughbridge was relatively brief.

Mrs Seaman, two doors up New Row from us, had evacuees from Newcastle despite having two children of her own, Barbara and Peter. I can't remember the names of the evacuees, but there was a lad about my age I started to play with. He was a nice friendly lad and I was getting on with him famously, but I very quickly picked up a Geordie accent from him which my mother thought was dreadful, so unfortunately the friendship was not encouraged. They too were not long before they returned home.

Later in the war during the time of the doodle bugs and V2s, there were further evacuees: Mrs Godley, her son Ron who was quite a talented artist, and her nephew Kenneth Lack. Their house in London had been bombed out, they had nowhere to live. They stayed until almost the end of the war. Kenneth was about my age, I made good friends with him. We wrote to each other very briefly after the war, he sent me a post card from his holiday in Hearne Bay, but to my regret the correspondence did not last and we lost touch.

Chapter 23. Personal Memories   Mike Tasker

Early School days

From our house in New Row, we used to take a short cut to school down the backs of New Row, through "Fanni's Alley", which ran through to St. James's Square, the passage is still there today although now blocked off by the Dining Room restaurant. Michael (and Brian) Fantini used to live there, Michael was my age and in our class at school, but suddenly the family disappeared, why I don't know, but it has occurred to me since that his family may have been interned, as many Italian families were as Italy entered the war. I have not been able to confirm this however. After they left the building was occupied by the army.

An enduring memory from the early days of the war was the Lord Kitchener's army recruitment poster above Benson's sweet shop in St. James's Square - it used to fascinate me. Kitchener's eyes would follow you all the way across the square wherever you went. I used to try to find a place where his eyes could not follow you – needless to say, there was nowhere.

On Aldborough Road heading towards school, we used to pass the army camp on the left (now housing). Dull red corrugated iron semi circular Nissen huts under tall trees with rooks nests, stretching down alongside Back Lane from York Road towards the Hall. I made friends from time to time with the soldiers there, but being a transit camp they never stayed long. I do remember one of the soldiers letting me play with his rifle – no bullets around of course, but great fun for a small boy. An early memory was that two boys in our class Eric Cousins and Peter Ellison (Squib) somehow managed to acquire some live bullets, causing great excitement amongst classmates. The army stores nearby were obviously not as secure as they should have been – well, that's how it was in war-time. I do remember later in the war removing the lead bullet from the cartridge, placing the bullet casing in our workshop vice and hitting the percussion cap with a hammer and nail. Whew! What an exciting bang. Health and Safety was but a futuristic concept at that time, and so it stayed until many years after the war.

I was blissfully unaware of the battle of Britain at the time, although there were always aeroplanes around. Dishforth was a very active airfield, as was Linton on Ouse, not very far away. There was certainly plenty of enemy action over the area particularly in 1941. The air raid warning siren was kept in the police station on the opposite side of the road from our house. The sound was deafening, it was so near. It sounded off many times, particularly in the early days of the war. It's strange what you can get used to. We had a corrugated iron air raid shelter in the garden, but it was dug deep into the clay about six feet into the ground. It would perhaps have offered some protection if the need had arisen, the trouble was, when it rained it filled with water. Fortunately it was never needed, so we were spared the choice between drowning or being bombed.

Mock Battles

The army used to have mock battles in and around the town from time to time, about the time of the D-Day landings. For a schoolboy returning from school, with all the bangs and flashes these were really exciting. One day as I passed Benson's sweet shop opposite the fountain, there was a soldier in full battle dress lying on the path in front of the shop, reading a sexy book while the bangs and flashes of a mock battle were going on all around him. I asked him what he was doing lying down there on the path. "I've been shot" he replied as he buried his head again in his Hank Janson book. Well how do you pass the time when you've been "shot", waiting for the battle to finish?

Occasionally there would be manoeuvres or similar happenings in the night, and it was not uncommon to see flares lighting up the night sky, floating down on small parachutes. One day I found one, I think it had landed in the Parochial Hall yard, a favourite playground for us. Great find! They were super to play with, to attach a stone to the bottom and throw up in the air and watch them float gently down. However, my throwing became too ambitious, the parachute finished up in a sycamore tree at the edge of the Parochial Church Hall yard. I thought I could recover it, so with some difficulty I climbed the tree, the parachute was on a branch some 20 feet above the ground with another branch about 4-5 feet below. I climbed along with my feet on the lower branch and my hands on the upper branch. Just as I stretched out to reach for the parachute, the lower branch shot away from my feet leaving me suspended in mid air hanging on with just my hands. My feet were now too far away from the lower branch, my arms gave way and I dropped to the ground some 20 feet below. I suppose I was lucky in that I only finished up with a badly sprained ankle and not a broken neck. I told my mother that I had stumbled over the wall, much lower. She was never sympathetic if she found out we were doing things she thought were wrong – at best we would get a good telling off, at worse a smack across the buttocks with the back of a hair brush.

The Black Bull

Many French Canadians were based at Dishforth, and the Black Bull seemed to attract quite a number of them for their nights out. One night I was in bed in our house just up the road in New Row, just about to go to sleep and suddenly lots of noise erupted down the street outside the Black Bull. A fight had broken out between French Canadians and the locals. I don't know what the outcome was, but a few days later there was a thousand bomber raid on Germany and very few of the French Canadians came back.

Flying Bomb

Late in the war after the V1s and V2s were landing on London, the siren went off one night in the police station opposite, we hadn't heard it much for some time. A local resident, I believe it was one of the postmen, said he had seen "a flying bomb, looked just like a flying telegraph pole!". I think he must have been very drunk, Boroughbridge was miles out of range, but who knew what the Germans had up their sleeve at that time, it could have been true. In fact, as it turned out, Boroughbridge was *not* out of range: the Germans had modified Heinkel 111 bombers to carry and launch the flying bombs, which they used to attack Manchester.

Plane Crash at Aldborough

News of the crashed Lancaster bomber at Aldborough on the 2nd of February 1944 buzzed around the lads in the town, and of course it was not long before we were up there at the scene of the crash. A prized possession at the time was a piece of perspex from a crashed plane, you could mould it into all sorts of shapes with a red hot poker, it was known and prized as a new wonder material. Sure enough I was able to find a piece from the wreckage of the cockpit canopy. I took it home and used a red hot poker to make a ring from it. At school we compared our mouldings - mine was nowhere near the best. That was the sort of thing we got a kick from at that time.

The crew of the plane were all tragically killed, I did hear that some of them had baled out, but they were too low, their parachutes failed to open in time. One of them I was told dropped on the cricket field. There was no sign of casualties when we arrived at the scene, just an RAF guard who did not stop us from collecting fragments of perspex.

Chapter 23. Personal Memories — Mike Tasker

Maple Leaf incident

After VE day, as a celebration of the allied victory, a group of Canadian Soldiers decided they would climb up on to the roof of the Fountain and leave a huge Maple Leaf, the Canadian National Symbol there before they departed for home.

A small crowd gathered and marvelled as the Canadians climbed up on to each other's shoulders. I think there were perhaps four soldiers in this chain until they reached the guttering of the roof. Quite a breath-taking sight. Much to everyone's horror, the guttering gave way and the top soldier came crashing down, fortunately he landed on the back of one of the soldiers beneath. He was badly shaken, but I don't think he suffered a lasting injury, nor did the soldier he fell on to. It would certainly have been a tragedy if he had fallen on to the hard steps below after surviving the war. I did not see them finally make it on to the roof, but the next day, sure enough, there was the Maple Leaf on the Fountain roof. It stayed there for quite a while afterwards, quite a fitting reminder of the Canadian presence in the area during the war.

Prisoner of War

My father had been posted to Newcastle in April 1942, not into the military, but to painting submarines in the Vickers Armstrong shipyards. He was released to return back home in December 1944. He worked at Dishforth for a while and was involved in some capacity supervising German POWs. This continued until after the war had finished and I remember him coming home one day with a German POW, Helmut, who came to help him do some gardening. It was the first time I had seen a German, the people we had learned to hate, but this guy seemed to be a really nice chap, tall and handsome and very easy to talk to, far from the Nazi stereotype we had had in mind. His English was excellent, and I believe after the war when he returned home, he became a town Bürgermeister (Mayor). He taught me my first word of German. My father had told him I wanted to know some German words. My eye caught my bike leaning against the wall outside our back door, so I asked him the German word for "bicycle". "Das Fahrrad" he answered, little could I know that that was my first word in a language which in later life preoccupied me for some 30 years.

Bridge Collapse

The story of the Great North Road bridge collapse in July 1945 is told in a previous chapter, p153. The Bailey Bridge, its immediate replacement, was not dismantled straight away after the old bridge was re-opened, and Colin and I used to take great delight in climbing amongst the bridge girders. Crossing from one side to the other along the roadway was boring for young lads, it was much more fun to cross by climbing through the girders on either side. We used to have races to see who could get across quickest.

I have vivid memories of my cub cap falling off one time as I clambered across, Colin saw it fall into the waters below, quickly clambered down and waded into the water in search of the cap. It had of course long since disappeared by the time he got down there – but Colin seemed completely oblivious of the dangers of the river at that point as he waded about looking for my cap. It could have been a total tragedy but, as young children are, no thought of danger entered our heads at the time. I don't know what cock and bull story we told my mother about the loss of the cub cap, she certainly never got to know the truth. She was not daft though, I suspect she didn't really believe what we told her anyway.

Barbara Breckon

The following memories were taken from a phone interview with Barbara Breckon, née Seaman, in June 2013.

Barbara does voluntary work at the Nidderdale Museum at Pateley Bridge, and is involved in historical research and genealogy. She also helps her eldest daughter, Dawn Haida, to record local MIs (missing individuals), and visits archives in North and West Yorkshire, Teesside and London regularly.

Barbara's father Walter Seaman was employed as civilian engineer at Dishforth from about 1938 until his death on 19th May 1955 (see photo, p113).

Evacuees and lodgers

Mrs Seaman took in many evacuees and lodgers throughout the war. Evacuees were from Liverpool, Newcastle and London.

"I remember a family from London, two boys I think, and there was a girl named Daphne who caused Mum and Dad a lot of worry – she was always getting into trouble and they all brought nits with them, and had only the clothes they stood up in!

Jim and Norma Sprung evacuated from Liverpool. Jim's family had an abattoir there. They lodged with Mum and Dad and, I think, for a while with Taylors, next door to Ramsdales butchers. They returned to Liverpool before the end of the war and Mum and Dad thought they had been killed in the blitz. Then the day my Dad died (19th May 1955) Mum and I had just returned from the hospital and there was a knock on the door and there stood Jim Sprung, passing through and looking-up Mum and Dad – what emotion, surprise, pleasure, shock and such sadness. Later that summer Jim and Norma (by then living in Ramsbottom) took us on holiday to their caravan in Wales. They had no family."

Bank manager George Smailes's wife was local Billeting Officer, responsible for allocating accommodation for evacuees. "She was I think connected with the WVS and I also think Dr. Rust's wife was very involved with the war effort." Barbara thinks George Dean also had some involvement with evacuees, and possibly also with the Air Raid Wardens.

Mrs Seaman also took in lodgers from RAF Dishforth, mostly officers who had batmen who cleaned up and made the bed – saving Mrs Seaman a job. "We did have some RAF men stay but on second thoughts I think most of the ones who had 'batmen' were Army personnel. I remember soldiers coming from the Old Hall near the bottom square (which was requisitioned during the war) to clean up after the Officers and polish their shoes, buttons etc, clean the bath, and make their bed."

Target practice

"I have vivid memories of soldiers lying on their stomachs (in full combat dress and helmets) in the passage of Beech House (Barbara's home in New Row) and firing out of the front door into sandbags placed at the bottom of the Police Station wall opposite. But I cannot believe that this would really have happened!"

A WAAF's baby

Barbara remembers in particular a Betty Grey, a WAAF at Dishforth. Unmarried, she had a baby, very much frowned upon at that time. Betty stayed with Seamans before and after the birth. When she started in labour Mrs Seaman went with her in a Reads taxi very late one night to a military hospital at Stockheld Park to have the baby. "I remember Mum saying what a really foggy night it was and she thought they were never

Chapter 23. Personal Memories   John Chippendale

going to get there in time and of course it was the wartime blackout which made night travel particularly difficult. The baby was a boy, Tony, he would be a bit younger than my brother Peter, and Mum passed all her baby clothes etc to Betty who had very little money.".

Loss of a godfather

One of the RCAF officers who stayed with Mrs Seaman was a French Canadian, Marcel, "a pilot in 61 Caribou Squadron flying Halifax bombers." Marcel was godfather to Barbara's brother Peter, but he was killed in action before the end of the war. "I was most upset as he had promised to bring me a monkey back from Canada after the war!"

Peter's christening, 3/11/1943, (left) with godfather Marcel and mother Elizabeth, (right) with godfather Marcel, godmother Betty Gray, and two other RAF friends.

John Chippendale

John Chippendale lived at 14 Springfield Road, Boroughbridge. There were houses on the left hand side of this road (town side), but opposite was rough ground, no houses. Then beyond this was a hedge and then Sadler's field (now Ladywell Road) with a pond more or less opposite where John lived. John wrote up some of his experiences in a newspaper article.

Source: Susan Robinson

I was almost six when war was declared in 1939, and eleven when the VE and VJ days came in 1945. Those six war years brought many changes to my small home town of Boroughbridge.

The town population was increased rapidly by the early establishment of an army camp in the hall grounds, with a subsidiary camp along from Springfield Road. Army manoeuvres occurred all around us, and particularly an assault course was constructed on waste ground immediately opposite my home. One returned from school to find thunder-flashes going off as recruits did crawls under barbed wire, scaled high plank walls or balanced their way across logs over deep pits. Of course it was a boy's delight to attempt the course when it was not being used by the military!

Boroughbridge is three miles south of Dishforth Aerodrome, and we had to take air-raid precautions seriously. The siren was on a pole also outside the police station, and in the early years of the war there were a number of alerts. We all carried gas masks to school in cardboard containers, which rapidly disintegrated and were replaced by canvas ones. Babies were provided with a "lie-in" mask and air was pumped to them via the filter using little hand-bellows. Pictured is my brother Chris, aged eleven at the time, pumping air to our nine month old brother Michael.

Elizabeth Thompson and Sheila Keighley

Elizabeth and Sheila, both nee Smailes, were daughters of George Smailes, the manager of Barclays Bank, Boroughbridge branch, and Mary Smailes, who was responsible for placing evacuees and for notifying families of deaths and injuries in service—two difficult and responsible jobs.

Source: Letter to author, from Elizabeth and Sheila, November 2013.

Chapter 23. Personal Memories — Elizabeth Thompson and Sheila Keighley

Mary, Sheila, George and Elizabeth Smailes

Elizabeth

I have very strong memories of the evacuees as my mother Mary was the Billeting Officer for Boroughbridge.

She had two families billeted on us, the first a mother and a daughter, early in the war – Mrs Perfect and Norma, they didn't stay long, Mr Perfect was in a munitions factory in London, and they all missed each other, so in the end mother and daughter returned home.

Later during the Doodlebugs in London we had Mrs Wainman, a little girl called Patricia whom I kept in touch with until I went to New Zealand. Also there was a baby whom I loved to bath after I came home from school. Many children came on their own from Leeds and the North East and were billeted on local families. Not easy, either for the children or for the families they were billeted on.

Looming large in my memory were the Lesser family, an elderly mother and father and several grown up daughters who suddenly arrived from London. They came from Germany in the thirties, I think they were Jewish. One of the daughters was married to a Sergeant Nussbaum, stationed at Dishforth and in the RAF Band. My mother had to find them somewhere to live. There was an empty pub on Horsefair, long since demolished [ed: the Royal Oak]. By the generosity of local families it was furnished for them and they moved in, but were not happy, they found all the army traffic very disturbing. My mother eventually found them a billet at Roecliffe. I do strongly recall coming home on more than one occasion to find them all sitting around our dining room table having tea – I don't know how she fed them all.

My mother was also the SSAFA representative (Soldiers, Sailors, Airmens Family Association) and had to go to Dishforth when there were bereavements and casualties. Her job was to contact and console the families of the bereaved, not an easy job.

There was a First Aid post in the gatehouse of the Three Arrows Hotel and we used to go to roll bandages etc there once a week. Mrs Nancy Rust, a retired nurse like my mother, was in charge of the volunteers there.

We lived at the Vineries off Horsefair via Cherry Lane next to Mr Hawking's pig farm. I went to school at Chatsworth House run by Mrs Hawking and daughter Muriel [ed: aunt and cousin of the famous Professor Stephen Hawking]. The outside privy was a bone of contention between my mother and Mrs Hawking, we were not allowed to use the WC inside and my mother wouldn't let me use the privy outside, so I had to run home when I needed to "go"!

The people I remember most clearly were Mr and Mrs Topham at the Post Office with their eleven children. Mrs Topham used to put on concerts at the Parochial Hall with the local children; the Army often took part too.

I remember dear Mr Potter at the hardware shop on the corner of Fishergate and Horsefair; Mrs Burley at her grocers on Horsefair with sacks of flour and tins of biscuits on the floor in front of the counter; Mr Burley, the butcher in the High Street; Mrs Davey at the Chocolate Buffet on Fishergate; Mrs Walton at the Green Grocers; Mr Ernie Robinson at the little Grocers on the corner of the High Street and the Square.

As my father worked in Barclay's Bank we had to patronise the shopkeepers who banked with Barclays. That meant that the daily papers came from Tophams and the weekend ones and magazines came from Pybus's!

I remember "Charlie Gas" Reynard at the Gas Works; Arthur Buck at the forge—I spent many a happy hour watching him shoe horses and ponies; also the lady at the telephone exchange next to Bobby Wilson's shop in the High Street—I never saw her face as she had her back to the window, it was rumoured that she listened in to calls!

I remember Billy Sadler and Miss Harriet Sadler and Mary "the milk" Dodsworth, at the farm in the High Street. Mary walked all around the town with her milk can and delivered to the door, jug left outside on the step with a net cover with beads around the outside to stop it blowing off in the wind!

I would go to the cricket field down by the river, to watch my father and the rest of the team. They'd be in the Club House and all the creepy crawlies, "silver fish" etc in the kitchen.

I remember the POWs in the Nissen Huts on the York Road. Italians came first then the Germans. The Italians worked on the local farms after they surrendered 1943-44, they came on the school bus which I used after I was 11, and went to school in Harrogate, we had a gas burner on the back of the bus as there was no petrol, and I recall seeing it travelling alongside the bus after becoming "undone" going down the hill by the Knaresborough Golf Club! We were late to school that day.

My father was in the AFS (Auxilliary Fire Service). The Fire Station was on Horsefair behind the butchers. He and other volunteers spent one night a week on fire watching duties and also other times practicing how to put out fires.

Just two final memories, the first, standing outside our house and the ground was shaking and the sky to the East was very red. My father said the Luftwaffe were bombing York.

The second, standing at my bedroom window in the early hours of the morning and seeing one of the planes returning to Dishforth on fire and crashing in the direction of the brickworks at Roecliffe.

Again another memory I have: the army parading in Fishergate on Friday evenings and their bands, the Kings Own Scottish Borderers.

Sheila

My earliest memory was standing outside the house watching the bombers flying overhead en route for bombing missions over Germany from Dishforth, counting them, and next morning counting them home, always several missing, and some badly damaged and flying very low.

Taking shelter in the cellar after the Air Raid Warning under strict instructions not to move until All Clear sounded.

Taking part in concert Parties run by Violet Topham.

I clearly remember the Sausage Pies made by my mother from tinned sausages from America, the fat on the top of the tin made wonderful pastry! The supply depended on how many ships managed to run the gauntlet of the U-boats in the Atlantic.

Going shopping with my mother at Ernie Robinson's little shop in the square for our meagre rations and occasional treats from under the Counter. Hard to believe now but the Ration Books with their little squares were valuable.

Our evacuee Mrs Perfect with her little girl Norma. They didn't stay long, she couldn't stand the peace and quiet of the country, and went back home to London and its bombs!

The First Aid Post run by amongst many others Nancy Rust, Dr Rust's wife, a retired nurse like my mother.

The constant stream of evacuees waiting to see my mother as Billeting Officer, and their hosts not always happy with the arrangements. She walked miles to get them happily settled in all weathers, a thankless task.

Joyce (Pinkney) Coates

Bob Pinkney

The only public air raid shelter that I remember, apart from the one under the school field, was in the orchard down Mill Lane just below our house. It was a solid oblong brick building with a thick concrete roof and, I understand, was never used, with one exception when, after the siren, Ella Kitching from the flats behind the Blinking Owl came all dressed up and volubly complained that no one else was there.

Myndhurst on Bridge Street had converted a cellar into a shelter. It was accessed from inside the house with an outlet into the yard. I remember dashing round there with Mum during a daytime raid and seeing an aeroplane flying so low one could see the swastika.

Next to the Mill House was the old Malt House (now Bridge End flats). During the war it was used as a food store. Wagon loads of food coming by rail (delivered by Dad) and the wooden crates of corned beef, dried milk etc being moved up and down to the various floors on metal rollers.

The Goods Station was extremely busy and was serviced by three, sometimes four, wagons. Supplies to Dishforth Aerodrome came by rail (Dad had a special pass to allow him on to the Drome, as security was very tight). Bombs and ammunition also came by rail to be distributed to the dumps in the countryside, one being the woods at Pilmoor.

I remember soldiers being stationed at the Hall, the Three Horse Shoes and where Springfield Drive is now, and also they constructed the Bailey Bridge across the River from the Hall Grounds (later to prove invaluable when the river bridge collapsed).

Because we had a spare room and bedroom we had service men (and wives) billeted on us during the war both Army and Airforce. I can only remember the names of two, a Captain Craig of a highland regiment (they kept in touch up to Mum's death) and the last, Captain Jack Sharples and his wife, Kay. There were also some evacuees. Winders had two teenage London boys, who were quite a handful; minor misdemeanours being attributed to them, so relief all round when they returned home.

The Parochial Hall was opened for the troops some evenings with local ladies providing tea and cakes. I presume there were cards, dominoes, reading matter etc available. Every so often entertainment was put on, with Mrs Violet Topham being one of the main organisers. We children were schooled in songs and dances and mother came up with costumes etc. On these occasions the Hall was packed and the shows were very well received. (I suppose we reminded them of their own children left at home.)

A Baby Clinic was started up by volunteers, namely Mrs Winder, Mrs Shipley, Mrs Frape, Mrs Summers and my Mum. It was held on Friday afternoons in the chapel School room, with a visiting Nurse and Doctor in attendance, in order that babies could be regularly checked; vaccinations given; and powdered milk and free concentrated orange juice was available.

We all had blackout curtains at the windows. Jonny Pickering, the cobbler was the warden, who soon came knocking at the door with a reprimand if half an inch of light was visible from outside.

Everyone had ration books for food and clothing, so it was a time of make do and mend.

Decorating seemed to consist of painting over existing wallpaper with coloured distemper.

We kept a pig, as did many people, so when it was killed it provided much extra food, shared with neighbours who in turn reciprocated. I can remember sides of bacon wrapped in muslin hanging from hooks in the kitchen ceiling. They were taken down and examined regularly in case flies had been around. The bacon was very salty! Eggs were mostly a dried powder, but any fresh ones obtained were preserved in Waterglass. Custard was made with cornflower, with colour and flavour added from a small bottle.

Coupons were swapped and bartered to enable ladies to get ingredients for baking and sugar to make jam. Everyone was positively discouraged from taking sugar in tea!

Flour was delivered to bakers in coarse linen type sacks. Empty sacks were in demand. They were bleached and made into pillow cases, cushion covers, etc and embroidered so they didn't appear so "utility".

Dances were held in the Crown Hotel, to which local girls were invited but not local boys, which caused some ill feeling and a few fights.

Aidan Foster

Aidan was born in Minskip in 1934, and moved to Langthorpe in 1938. He was 5 years old at the outbreak of the war. He went to Kirby Hill school which was almost within sight of Dishforth Aerodrome, so was witness to several flying incidents in the vicinity—more of which later.

A memory from the early part of the war, was of a large army convoy arriving in the area, going down Dog Kennel Lane with huge field guns, which they deployed in Dennis Gill's field. Aidan and his pals went down there on their bikes to see what was going on. In retrospect Aidan thinks this was part of army defensive manoeuvres, aimed at forming an effective defensive line at a period when there was a real possibility of a German invasion. The army camped out in the nearby fields during these operations, and part of the encampment was a tented canteen. They stayed there for about three weeks. Aidan remembers, as they left, they handed out items of foodstuff they no longer needed and one of Aidan's abiding memories was a can of marmalade as big as a bucket which came his way, along with tins of bully beef and other food items. Surplus food was handed out to the locals—more than welcome in those times of shortages and food rationing.

Aidan's most poignant memory is of the Army building Bailey bridges across the river Ure at the far end of Langthorpe. In retrospect this was clearly preparation for the follow up to the D-Day landings in June 1944 and the liberation of France. He remembers lots of soldiers from the Royal Engineers from Ripon arriving with cranes and lorry loads of bridge building equipment. He watched them unloading the pontoons which, because of their length, were delivered in two halves. They were taken to the river and then, once afloat, bolted together. As they added the pontoons in this way metal girder framework sides and base were built up, and on reaching the other side a track was laid across as a road surface. Once this was complete the army would run tanks, Bren gun carriers, sometimes field guns across to the other side and back again. Once this had been done successfully they would dismantle the bridge and return with all the equipment to their base in Ripon. This as Aidan remembers they repeated at least four times, each time the operation lasted about a week On one of these practices they carried out the

Chapter 23. Personal Memories — Aidan Foster

operation in mock battle conditions, with gunfire, thunder flashes, explosions, smoke and noise of battle. So exciting for a young lad. Much of this Aidan was able to watch from his bedroom window in his house just opposite.

Location of Bailey Bridges, still visible in 2015

Whilst assembled in the school playground ready to go into class, Aidan was witness to a particular air crash which remains a vivid memory for him. There was an aircraft approaching overhead with its engines misfiring and in obvious trouble. He saw the crew bail out even though it was quite low, but luckily they all survived. The unmanned plane did a half moon curl and unbelievably landed on its belly in a nearby field. One of the crew landed in the school grounds. The rest of the crew quickly gathered together and returned to Dishforth, obviously shaken, but uninjured.

A further incident Aidan witnessed early in the war was the mysterious landing of an Auster light aircraft which landed in a field behind the council houses between Langthorpe and Kirby Hill. A car drew up nearby and people got out, the crew climbed out of the plane, There was a brief meeting, maps and papers were exchanged, the pilot took off in the plane and the car drove away. Aidan has pondered ever since about what was going on with this strange event—could they have been spies?—were they practicing for some sort of SOE (Special Operations Executive) mission over occupied Europe?—or was it just a delivery of routine papers? We will never know.

Evacuees were accommodated in Langthorpe as in the rest of the area, particularly in the early years of the war. Anyone with spare rooms had to take them in. Aidan came down for his breakfast one day to find two girls at the breakfast table! "Who are these girls?" he asked his mother. "Evacuees", she replied. The police had arrived the previous night, knocked on the door and announced that these evacuees had to be accommodated, no choice. The girls did not stay long, stayed for a few weeks then went back home. There were several evacuees temporarily at Kirby Hill school, quite a number from Gateshead. It was obvious from their clothing that some of them came from a very poor background. Some of them had very poor clothes and they brought nits with them, and of course shared them with the rest of the class. [*Author's note:*

where have we heard that story before?] There were stories of "Nitty Norah, the bug explorer" who came to sort them out, using a special fine tooth comb to tease out the nits.

Aidan remembers that there was a Jewish couple who came just before the war, they stayed in a caravan throughout the war, in a field adjacent to Langthorpe houses which Aidan passed every day on his way to school. They were pleasant people who greeted the children as they passed. They had a sign on the caravan which said "Unter den Linden" - which is of course one of the most well known streets in Berlin, leading to the Brandenburg Gate. They very probably lived there before escaping to England before the war started. They were amongst the lucky ones who managed to escape from Germany before the Holocaust.

In the early hours of one morning in March 1945 Aidan remembers being woken up by air raid sirens and cannon fire. Two Canadian Halifax bombers were flying over, one already on fire, and another which burst into flames after a round of cannon fire. He and his friends cycled to the crash site, by Burton Grange Farm, between Langthorpe and Helperby, the next day. The aircraft had crashed upside down and all eight on board had died. Investigations showed it had been brought down by a Messerschmitt 110, probably during the Luftwaffe's final night-attack operation, on the night of 3rd-4th March 1945. Years after the war, in 1950, Aidan recovered an axe from the crashed bomber whilst ploughing the crash site. Eventually the axe was presented to the Royal British Legion in 2013.

Ken Needham

Ken was born in 1931. He lived in Langthorpe near the brewery. He was the same age as Aidan Foster, they were playmates, but lived at opposite ends of the village.

Ken remembers the pioneer corps digging holes and planting explosives on the iron railway bridge in preparation to blow up the bridge in the event of a German invasion. It must have been in 1940.

He also remembers the Brewery Yard buildings accommodating soldiers. He particularly remembers a sergeant being marched about, it appeared that he was on a "fizzer"—a charge for some misdemeanour.

Part of the brewery building was used as an emergency food store in the latter part of the war, and immediately post-war.

A POW worked for Cyril Middleton on the Kirby Hill road.

Audrey (Styan) Horton

During the war Audrey worked at Greenwood and Batley Bullet and Shell Factory, Farnham (see p116). Her recollections below are quoted from a letter, 9/4/2015.

"My father A V Styan and a neighbour A Kettleboro', both builders by trade, were recruited to work in London, restoring blitzed properties during 1943-44.

It was during 1944 that myself, a friend and my sister were cycling home (to Minskip) from a dance at Ouseburn, when a stray German plane machine gunned us. We were fortunate enough to jump into the hedge in time. We were attacked in broad moonlight on the road between Aldborough Cemetery and Stump Cross. What memories!"

Index

The following men and women are listed in the chapters on Active Service.

Akers
  Cpl Kenneth, 33
  Sgt Donald, 33
Allen
  Herbert, 62
Atkinson
  Ellen, 117
  Jack, 60
  Janet, 116
  Sergeant Roland Patrick (Paddy), 23
Ayres
  Billy, 62

Barugh
  Freda Elsie, 116
Baynes
  Vera, 104
  William, 17
Bendelow
  Thomas, 59
Benson
  Sgt John, 59
Berry
  Pte George J, 40
Binns
  Wilfred L "Whippet", 28
Blakeborough
  Tommy, 40
Boddy
  Charles, 19
Boddye
  Frank, 43
Bowes
  Lawrence (Lol), 47
Broadbelt
  Ordinary Seaman Robert, 11
Brown
  Johnny, 41
Burks
  Sgt Jack, 37

Burley
  Dorothy, 104
  Stan, 119
Burton
  Cliff, 60
Busby
  Ernest, 31

Calley
  Cliff, 24
Calvert
  Maurice, 29
  Sergeant Tom, 16
Campbell
  Bernard (Bunny), 38
  Edna, 105
  Kenny, 63
  Leslie W., 63
Capstick
  Billy, 113
  Jimmy, 22
Chipchase
  Eleanor, 116
Clayton
  Bernard, 43
  Bill, 37
  Captain John, 44
  Cpl Albert, 37
  Geoff, 44
  Gordon, 33
  Herbert (Bert), 36
  Isabelle (Belle), 102
  Mary, 116
  Sgt Geoffrey, 33
  Tom, 37
Clift
  Lance Corporal Jack Harrison, 21
  Percy, 21
Cooke
  Bill, 53
  Sgt Herbert, 53

Cooper
  Arthur, 58
  Ernest, 58
  Pte Harry, 17
  Robert, 58
Craggs
  Clare, 46
  Sapper Godfrey, 14
  Sapper Herbert, 45
Crozier
  Corporal Donald, 59
  Sergeant Gilbert, 17

Dagget
  Ruth, 103
Daniel
  Betty, 104
Darwin
  Captain Bobby, 47
Davy
  Joan, 102
Deighton
  Herbert, 62
Denny
  N F, 61
Derbyshire
  Gladys, 103
Dockray
  Sgt June, 103
Dodsworth
  Harry, 62
Duck
  Sgt Olive, 101

Eagle
  Joan, 104
Easton
  Robert, 58
Edwards
  Kath, 116
Evans
  H., 62

175

Farrar
  Bernard, 21
  Bernice, 104
  Reginald, 20
  Vincent, 21
Foster
  Ernest, 52, 107
  Sgt Maurice, 52
Frape
  Eric, 30

Gault
  Barbara, 104
  Olive, 104
  Sergeant Basil T, 11
Goodall
  Alan, 58
  Ken, 55
Green
  Sergeant Peter Harry
    Barrowclough (Barry), 16
Greensitt
  A., 119
  Frank, 42
  J., 62
Groves
  Bill, 48
Gudgeon
  Tom, 119

Hammond
  Cora (Herron), 115
  William "Wally", 34
Hannam
  Eric, 17
Harcourt
  Sgt Bernard, 38
Hare
  Cyril, 49
  Dennis, 49
  LAC Albert, 49
Harland
  Sgt Christopher William, 58
Hartley
  Gunner George (William Thomas), 12
  Herbert, 53
Hawking

Warrant Officer Henry
  Halton, 16
Hawkridge
  Annie, 103
  Madge, 116, 117
  W/Sgt Arthur, 51
Helm
  Lawrence, 119
Henderson
  Cpl James, 41
Henry
  Flight Lieutenant Michael Thomas Gibson, 18
Herron
  Charles Herbert, 35
  Fred, 35
  Sid, 35
  Winnie, 116
Holmes
  Joan, 100
Holtby
  Warrant Officer Maurice, 31
Horner
  Gunner Bob, 35
  Henry, 63
  Pte Cliff, 36
  RSM (Quartermaster) Sergeant Ron, 36
Hudson
  Lill, 116
Hughes
  Edna, 116
  George, 34

Ingledew
  Bill, 48
  John (Jack), 48

Jones
  Flight Lt Jack, 56

Keighley
  Captain Jack, 24
Kirby
  C. Dennis, 63
  Fred, 119
  Henry, 56
  Jenny, 116

Kitching
  Fusilier Vivian G, 13
  Harold, 39
  Owen, 39

Lambert
  Percy, 62
Large
  Reg, 27
Lawn
  Jimmy, 23
Lawson Tancred
  Flight Ltn Andrew Thomas, 14
  Henry and Christopher, 47
Lebert
  Cpl Alphonse Jack, 99
Leboeuf
  Ray, 99
Leckonby
  Earnest, 58
Lee
  Charlie, 52
Leeming
  Mavis, 116
  Tom, 31
Lees
  Captain Robert Ferguson, 13
Ligertwood
  Jean, 105
Lindsey
  Arthur, 41
  John, 41
  Walter, 62
Lofthouse
  Douglas (Doug), 19, 65–96
  Sgt Tom, 25
Lonsdale
  Alfred, 57
  Frank, 39
Lowther
  Ben, 42
  Conald "Con" Crosby, 50
  Harry, 42
Lumsden
  Jack, 31

176

Index

Malton
  Lillian, 103
Mawtus
  Geoff, 63
  Sgt Donald, 62
McKellah
  Vera, 116
Metcalfe
  Sgt Sidney, 51
Morgan
  Arthur, 58
Morrison
  Eddie, 54
Morten
  Stan, 29
Mudd
  Betty, 116
  Fred, 25
  Leslie, 22
Murdoch
  Sgt Don, 27
Myers
  Flight Sergeant Dennis, 11
  Major Norman, 59

Norfolk
  Eric Parker, 41

Others, 55

Peacock
  Pte Ronald "Roy", 58
  Stella, 117
Pearson
  Harold, 28
  Hugh, 29
  Roy, 119
Peleshok
  Warrant Officer Neil, 100
Perris
  Mary Olive, 103
Porter
  Cpl Raymond, 40
  Sgt Eddie, 40
Pratt
  Billy, 45
  Eric, 45
  Geoffrey, 15
  George, 60

Leslie, 14
Proctor
  Bill, 60
  Harry, 60
Pybus
  Squadron Leader Claude William Smith, 23

Rabbit
  Winnie, 116
Ramsdale
  Harry, 41
Reed
  Jenny, 116
  Richard "Sonny", 13
Rennison
  Arthur, 47
  Ernest, 46
Richardson
  Cpl Robert Edward (Bob), 30
  Ken (Gus), 19
  RSM Arthur, 30
  Winnie, 104
Richmond
  John (Jock), 27
Robinson
  Emily, 102
  Leonard, 32
  Pte Norman Spenton, 21
Robshaw
  Eileen, 115
  Joyce, 105
  Sgt Jack, 38
Robson
  Morris, 37

Sampson
  Ernest, 40
Sawford
  George, 40
Schofield
  Tommy, 53
  Walter, 53
Scott
  Clarence, 62
Seaman
  Walter, 113
Sharples

Captain Jack, 22
Slater
  Dennis, 33
Smart
  Lance Corporal William Edward, 18
Smith
  Billy, 39
  Les, 39
  Richard, 28
Spearman
  Bob, 38
Steele
  Sgt Fred, 25
  Thomas (Tony), 25
Stokes
  Sgt Alf, 26
Stubbs
  Freda, 117
Styan
  Audrey, 116, 174
  Malcolm Raymond, 61

Tasker
  Herbert, 114
Taylor
  Barbara, 103
  Corporal Richard, 15
  Jack, 39
  Phil, 40
  Roy, 39
  Violet, 117
Tennant
  Henry, 42
  James, 42
  Jenny, 117
Tew
  Sgt George William, 54
Thatcher
  Fred, 107
Thirkill
  Billy, 58
Thomas
  Jimmy, 34
Thompson
  Chrissie, 116
Thorpe
  Lawrence, 56

W. (Bill), 56
Tilburn
 Betty, 102
 Sergeant George H, 12
Tubby
 Donald, 49
 George, 16
 Levi, 49
 May, 102
 Petty Officer Harold, 16
 Reg, 50
Tucker
 Reg, 26

Varley
 Jack, 29

Waddington
 Margaret, 104
 Vera, 104
Waite
 Gladys, 116

Phyllis, 117
Sgt Herbert Ridley, 51
Walton
 Wing Commander
  Herbert, 24
Ward
 Joan, 102
 Norman, 32
 Stanley, 50
Wardell
 Alec, 52
 Sheila, 104
Wardley
 Betty, 101
Watson
 Cpl George, 20
 Eric, 20
 William, 28
Watts
 Evelyn, 105
 Tommy, 63
 Viera, 105

Violet, 103
Weaver
 Billy, 27
Weinhardt
 Horst, 109
Whiteley
 Tommy, 57
Whiting
 Frank, 56
Wilkinson
 Barbara, 104
Wilson
 Fred, 22
 Sgt Frank A, 38
Wombwell
 Henry, 28
Wrightson
 George, 57
 Jack, 57
Wynn
 John, 38

Made in the USA
Charleston, SC
25 November 2015